MANAGERIAL DECISION MAKING and LEADERSHIP

The Essential Pocket Strategy Book

MANAGERIAL DECISION MAKING and LEADERSHIP

The Essential Pocket Strategy Book

Caroline Wang

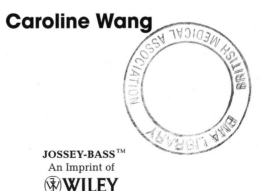

JOSSEY-BASS™
An Imprint of
WILEY

This edition is published in 2010 by John Wiley & Sons (Asia) Pte. Ltd., 2 Clementi
Loop, #02-01, Singapore 129809 on behalf of Jossey-Bass, A Wiley Imprint.
989 Market Street, San Francisco, CA 94103-1741–www.josseybass.com

Jossey-Bass books and products are available through most bookstores. To contact
Jossey-Bass directly, call our Customer Care Department within the US at 800-956-
7739, outside the US at 317-572-3986, or fax 317-572-4002.

Jossey-Bass also publishes its books in a variety of electronic formats. Some content
that appears in print may not be available in electronic books.

Library of Congress Cataloging-in-Publication Data

ISBN: 978-0-470-82525-9

Typeset in 10.5/14 point, Times Roman by MPS Limited, A Macmillan Company,
Chennai, India

Printed in Singapore by C.O.S Printers Pte Ltd
10 9 8 7 6 5 4 3 2

Contents

Preface

When I joined the workforce at IBM in the United States 30 years ago, the area of decision making greatly puzzled me. I did not have a good decision-making framework in the first decade of my career, and the quality of my decisions was hit and miss.

Sometimes I made decisions that had good outcomes, and that made me happy, but I could not explain what I had done to cause these desirable outcomes. I attributed them to others' advice, experience, my intuition, or luck. I was not confident that they could be repeated, neither could I explain the elements of a quality decision. Some of my decisions also resulted in challenges, difficulties, or undesirable outcomes.

So I reflected more deeply on what it takes to make quality decisions. What are the critical elements for good decisions and desirable outcomes? Could there be a simple and useful decision-making framework for all practical decisions, especially those that do not involve quantitative analysis (such as decisions related to human resources or customer relations)? I asked many successful people about how they made decisions—and interestingly, even today, I have not met anyone who can respond with a quick, crisp answer. Most people I asked would reply, "That's a tough question, let me think about it and get back to you later." Of course, most of them never got back to me. I did not find what I was looking for.

In my search for the important elements of quality decisions, in the early 1990s I attended a seminar called "Decision Quality" by Strategic Decisions Group, which pointed me in the right direction and provided the fundamental structure for my search. I am immensely grateful for it. Even though the seminar had more quantitative analysis than I needed, it started my pursuit of a decision-making framework that could be used for team decisions, especially non-quantitative decisions. It helped me to observe, think, experiment, and reflect on my own and others' decisions.

Every decision, small or large, became an opportunity to experiment, learn, and improve, as I tried to reduce this complex topic into some simple and easy-to-remember principles. Gradually, it was demystified, and more than a decade ago, I was able to simplify the decision-making framework into six easy-to-remember letters—GPA and IPO—in order to lead various teams to make decisions. The GPA IPO framework can be used in all sorts of managerial decisions, and can also be applied to personal decisions in everyday life. It has helped me to make quality decisions every time. Over the past decade, I only made two decisions that produced less than desirable outcomes (both personal investment decisions), and the reason the outcomes were poor was because I made those two decisions on my own, without involving the right participants. Basically, I did not practice what I preached in those two cases. They also proved that team decisions can be better than individual decisions, as long as the team uses a logical decision-making framework.

I worked at IBM for a quarter of a century before taking up my current position as a faculty member at the Hong Kong University of Science and Technology (HKUST). In that quarter-century, I rotated through 12 departments, including Sales, Services, Technical Support, Business Development, Consulting, Human Resources, Marketing, IBM Internal Transformation and Information Management. I was vice president of information technology and business transformation from late 1988 to

January 2000, responsible for IBM's Y2K transition in Asia Pacific, and vice president of marketing from January 2000. I started in the US and spent the first 15 years there; then I was transferred to Tokyo and worked there for seven years before being transferred to China (Hong Kong). I was IBM's vice president of marketing for Asia Pacific (including such countries and areas as Japan, Korea, Greater China, Southeast Asia, India, Australia and New Zealand) in late 2003 when I was appointed adjunct professor by HKUST to teach its MBA and Executive MBA program in the School of Business and Management.

Whenever I was asked how I could survive and succeed while working in such highly diversified environments and leading multicultural teams, my answer was, "I know how to lead a team to make the best decisions for the company and to implement the decisions successfully." This should be the textbook answer for all managers and leaders. I was parachuted into different management positions to lead multicultural teams in different fields, yet it always took just a short period of time for me to gain trust from the teams to achieve our shared goals— because I made my decision-making framework public. Without losing control or reducing my own responsibility for the decisions, I allow the entire team to also take ownership of the decisions.

If GPA IPO is mastered, any manager or leader can lead their teams with confidence to make the best decisions and to successfully execute them.

CAROLINE WANG
Hong Kong
May 1, 2010

Introduction

Successful organizations rely on competitive products and services to excel in the marketplace. Internally, quality managerial decision making is necessary to create and sustain this success. Managers face different challenges every day, and their decision-making ability determines how successful the organization, and their own careers, can be in the long term. Quality decision making is thus a competence that every responsible manager must acquire, and a discipline that must be practiced.

This book attempts to simplify a seemingly complicated issue: how managers can make responsible decisions of all types at all times. Most people believe the myth that there can be no common decision-making framework for all decisions, because every decision is unique and every decision maker is unique. However, a common framework for the thought process of decision making is, in fact, possible. This book lays out a straightforward decision-making framework for any manager to use when leading his or her team to make quality decisions that achieve organizational goals. The framework is practical and easy to remember, and although it is not necessarily easy to implement in the beginning, it becomes easier with practice.

This book places emphasis on leading a team to make decisions, even though the framework can also be used for personal and individual decisions. Efficient and effective team decision making has always been a challenge; moreover, team decision making often does not necessarily lead to higher quality decisions, despite the effort spent. The framework shared in this book does not use a voting system that allows majority rule, nor is it a consensus decision-making process in which any member can veto the decision. The leader of the team is the decision maker, and has to bear final responsibility for the decision. However, he or she can learn who to invite into the decision-making process and how to lead the process to maximize the quality and "executability" of the final decision.

Furthermore, using the GPA IPO framework, the leader can gain confidence and team support for the decision, will be able to articulate and defend the decision, and will have made the necessary preparations for successful implementation when the decision-making process is complete. The framework should be shared with all team members to get their "buy-in" and to increase the credibility of the leader and his or her final decisions. And, of course, team members can use the framework to make their own decisions, and can be confident in sharing the process and outcome of their decisions with anyone who has questions. This decision-making framework can align the team, improve teamwork and increase the odds of success during the implementation stage.

Office politics, which are often the result of subordinates' ignorance of how managers make decisions, can be eliminated as well. When subordinates do not know how leaders make decisions, they are likely to build fawning relationships with their superiors in the hope of lobbying them to make decisions that favor them personally. Such lobbying is a hindrance to the organization.

In Joel Brochner's *Harvard Business Review* article "Why It's So Hard to Be Fair" (March 2006), he made a strong case for process fairness in addition to outcome fairness. It's difficult to be perceived as fair, even if the outcome is fair, when the decision-making process is opaque. It pays, therefore, to make the process transparent and to involve the team members in it. Using a public decision-making framework means that the entire team can make quality decisions, and that all team members are liable for the consequences of the decisions made. This guards against "us versus them" attitudes developing between team members and managers.

All responsible leaders and managers should be willing and able to share how they make decisions. I have read and heard of many successful leaders who attribute their good decisions to intuition—but if one's intuition has no pattern, it is sheer luck. We can envy this luck, but there is nothing for us to learn from. Managers who have become successful through intuitive decision making add no lasting value to the organization because they make no contribution to organizational capability or sustainability. At most, such managers can boast about their "special sense;" and make themselves indispensable.

Managerial decision making is not a one-time event; it is part of the journey of continuous learning and improvement. **Observe, think**, and **experiment** are the three critical steps in this journey. The total outcome of managerial decisions can be optimized by the continuous improvement process.

Some managers use a democratic voting system to make decisions. I personally only use voting to make quick and insignificant decisions, such as which restaurant we go to for our next team dinner. I do not use voting for significant business decisions, because decisions made by a vote have three drawbacks:

1. They are not fair. Not all voters are equally qualified to evaluate the choices, and the decision will affect voters in differing degrees. Therefore, it is not fair to treat all votes with equal weight and to use a one-person, one-vote system for making final decisions.

2. Everyone, including the leader, can hide behind a democratic voting system to escape individual responsibility. The majority

can say, "It wasn't just me, it was the majority," and the minority can say, "I told you so, I opposed the choice."

3. After democratic voting the team is divided, not united. People tend to take sides even after the voting is complete, and this decreases the odds of successful implementation, because part of the team feels overruled. Then the leader needs to spend additional time and effort to unite the team and obtain their "buy-in" before the decision can be successfully implemented.

Some managers get so frustrated with democratic debates—which can be irrational, emotional, and unproductive—that they just make decisions by themselves. However, this creates a very passive work environment in which the employees do not feel that they need to bear any responsibility, because they just do what the boss tells them to do. It also leaves the boss exhausted and wondering why no one is proactive or takes responsibility for the organization.

Work time is an organizational asset, not an individual one. The organization exchanges its financial resources for the work time of its employees. An employee's time is the most finite, non-renewable corporate resource. Everything must be accomplished with time and in time, and thus every employee is a decision maker, since he or she is the person who actually allocates the organization's most finite resource. Having all members of an organization repeatedly and habitually making good decisions can therefore be a powerful competitive advantage. An outstanding manager should therefore focus on improving the team members' abilities to make quality decisions.

If a quality decision-making framework is learned and used by all members of the organization, they can all make quality decisions even in the absence of the manager, and the success of the organization can be sustained. Using a publicly shared decision-making framework can thus increase the productivity of the organization by minimizing guesswork.

This book outlines what I have learned from the observe-think-experiment cycle when leading various multicultural, multi-functional teams to make the best decisions for achieving organizational goals. My intent is not to give individuals a "secret weapon" for success, but to allow all professional managers to guide their teams to make the best decisions for the organization. This book does not discuss *what* the best decisions to make are; it shares a decision-making framework that can help each manager and leader to know *how* to lead a team to make the best decisions.

Note that I use the terms "leader" and "manager" interchangeably throughout the book. This is because I believe that a good leader does not only lead but also manages, and a good manager not only manages but also leads.

Good decision-making frameworks can result in using the organization's finite resources in the most efficient and effective way to achieve its goals.

THE GPA IPO FRAMEWORK

A quality decision requires content quality and process quality. **Goal**, **Priorities**, and **Alternatives** (GPA) are the three key elements for content quality.

The abbreviation GPA happens to stand for "grade point average" in the US grading system. If we were to give our own or another's decision a grade, what grading standard should we use? How should we evaluate the quality of a decision? We can use GPA—we can evaluate the quality of a decision by the quality of its goal, priorities, and alternatives:

- Is the **goal** clear and shared by all team members?
- Is proper **priority** given to different matters—i.e. are we focusing on the most important matter first?
- Do we have enough innovative and implementable **alternatives** to achieve our goal?

Information, **People**, and **Objective reasoning** (IPO) are the three key elements for process quality. IPO happens to stand for "initial public offering" as well. I put the three elements in this sequence because

1) it is easy to remember, and 2) the acronym reminds us that during the decision-making process, we need to prepare to change our decision in the future—just as a share price changes immediately after it is listed on the IPO opening day, even though the initial price was chosen carefully after a long decision-making process. Since all decisions are about the future, we should not be overconfident and believe that the current decision is so good that it will never need to be changed. It will be changed—either by us or by others—and it is better if it is the former.

These three elements influence the efficiency and effectiveness of the decision-making process, as well as the final outcome of the decision, especially during the execution/implementation stage. We need to ask the following questions to obtain process quality:

- What kind of **information** is needed to proactively adjust our decision in the future in order to achieve the best outcome over time?
- **Who** should participate in the decision-making process to increase decision quality and the odds of successful implementation?
- How can we choose the best alternative through **objective reasoning** to make the best decision?

The order in which we deal with these three questions is not as important as ensuring that each question has been satisfactorily answered.

In the nine chapters of this book, I outline the GPA IPO elements for leading a team to make quality decisions. Chapter 1 defines "decision" and many other terms that will appear frequently throughout the book. Chapter 2 covers a number of the traps that can derail the quality decision-making process. Chapter 3 moves into the GPA half of the framework and discusses G—the goal which should always be the starting point of a quality decision. Chapter 4 is on priorities, often the most difficult dimension of a decision, and Chapter 5 is on alternatives, the most innovative part of a decision. The following three chapters deal with my second mnemonic device for the process side of decision making: IPO. Chapter 6 deals with objective reasoning, which usually takes the most time in the decision-making process. Chapter 7 talks about information, and Chapter 8 concludes the second section with a discussion of the people involved in decision making and the leadership styles needed for effective decision making. Finally, Chapter 9 provides concluding comments and offers some parting advice.

CHAPTER 1

Decisions and Decision Making

Why do we need to make decisions? Well, we don't need to make decisions unless we are faced with the following three conditions:

1. We have choices.
2. We have finite resources which prevent us from pursuing all the choices simultaneously.
3. We have a goal to achieve.

If we have no goal—that is, if we do not really know what we want at the end or where we are going—then it does not matter which choice we select. If we have infinite resources, then we can implement all our choices at once. If we know the goal we are aiming at and have finite resources, but only have one feasible option for achieving our goal, we cannot make a decision about whether we will take this sole option or not. But if all three conditions are met, we need to choose the alternative that best enables us to achieve our goal within the constraints of our resources.

Why is decision making so difficult? Because all decisions are about the future, and the future offers no facts—the future and facts are mutually exclusive. History cannot be changed, but the future will be determined by our decisions. And since there are no facts about the future, we can only make decisions based on our assumptions about the future. We do not have a crystal ball in which to see the future.

The future and facts are mutually exclusive

Scientific facts about the universe may be projected forward into the future much more accurately than facts regarding human actions. Anything man-made can be changed, so while our assumptions can be based on an educated guess, we must allow for uncertainty and risk management in our decision-making process. No one should be so confident of his or her decisions as to be closed to suggestions for change. It is better if we proactively monitor our own decisions and take the initiative to make adjustments as needed, rather than wait for someone else to force a change on us due to our inertia.

Now let's begin this chapter's examination of decisions and decision making by defining some terms that will appear frequently throughout this book:

- **Decision**—resource allocation (including tangible and intangible resources).*
- **Decision maker**—the person who allocates resources.
- **Strategy**—a set of implementable decisions and policies that have long-term impact.*
- **Decision-making process**—choosing the best alternative for accomplishing goals with finite resources.
- **Strategic decisions**—choosing the right road to run on.*
- **Operational decisions**—running well on the chosen road.*

---

*The terms marked with an asterisk were defined by the Strategic Decisions Group for their seminars on decision quality.

Quality decisions are made by people who are "willing" and "able":

- **Willing**—the decision maker wants to make quality decisions. It often takes courage to be willing.
- **Able**—the decision maker knows how to make quality decisions. Skills and resources enable the decision maker to make quality decisions.

In the rest of this chapter, we'll look at these terms in a little more detail.

WHAT IS A DECISION?

A decision is not merely a discussion, an order, an agreement, or a compromise—a decision should not be discussed as if it is only a noun. A decision should be discussed as a verb. A decision is a specific allocation of resources. A decision is to be executed, and it takes resources to execute. No resource allocation means no real decision has been made. There can be no real changes without changes of resource allocation.

So, decisions should be regarded as allocations of real resources, whether tangible or intangible. Decision and execution should be seen as two parts of a whole; if there is no execution, then the decision was just a slogan. Decision makers should not separate the decision and the execution in their thought process, even if someone else will be undertaking the execution—they should not say, "My decision was good, but the execution was poor," if the decision fails in the execution stage. A decision is for its execution, and its execution is for achieving the goal of the decision. So, the decision maker must be prepared for the consequences of his or her decision when it is executed.

Sometimes an issue is discussed multiple times at management meetings, yet no outcome, no progress, and no change actually takes place. If you dig a little deeper, you will find that this is because no resources were allocated to the issue or no changes were made in resource allocation.

Decisions are made only when resources are allocated

Decisions are made only when resources are allocated. Decisions need to be executed; good execution achieves the goal of the decision by using finite resources efficiently and effectively.

As mentioned earlier, a decision is all about choosing the best alternative to achieve a goal with finite resources, whether tangible or intangible. Tangible resources are quantifiable resources, such as time, money, patents, intellectual property, and fixed assets. Intangible resources are resources that are not yet quantifiable, but have the potential to become tangible resources, like brand image, reputation, credibility, knowledge, talent, and skills. For instance, a celebrity with a very positive public image can turn this intangible resource into a lucrative advertising contract, which is a quantifiable tangible resource. A company can turn its valuable brand image into premium pricing. In the same way, a leader can use his or her name as executive sponsor to support a certain project. Even though the leader may not be involved to the extent of allocating tangible resources (i.e. time and money), his or her image and credibility is drawn upon. This allocation of intangible resources can trigger the allocation of tangible resources by others, and increase the odds of success for the project. However, if the project ends in disaster, it will tarnish the figurehead leader's reputation and decrease his or her intangible resources. So, even intangible resources are finite and subject to depletion.

WHO IS THE DECISION MAKER?

The decision maker is the one who allocates resources—the one who is willing and able, and actually allocates resources. Sometimes, the person who acquires the resources and the person who allocates the resources are different—as in a family, where one spouse may be the breadwinner while the other manages the family budget and does all the shopping. The one who actually allocates the resources (does the shopping) is the decision maker.

If we do not possess all the resources needed to implement a decision, we must identify and gain the support of the appropriate decision maker in the organization—the person who is both willing and able to allocate the resources needed. (As mentioned previously, in some ways, all members of an organization are decision makers, as they allocate both their own time at work and the corporate resources they are authorized to distribute.)

We might say that a rich person who does not spend money and a poor person who has no money to spend are equal, in a way, in that neither makes purchasing decisions. Perhaps the rich person has more potential to become a decision maker, as he or she is more able to purchase; yet the poor person may well be more willing to purchase—and at the end of the day, where there is a will, there is a way. The poor person could borrow money to make the purchase, whereas the rich person might never buy the product because he or she is unwilling to allocate resources to a product that he or she does not like.

WHAT IS STRATEGY?

Strategy is a set of specific decisions and policies that specify implementable management actions and have long-term results, according to the Strategic Decisions Group. In other words, strategy is a series of resource allocations designed to reach a specific goal that has long-term significance.

THE DECISION-MAKING PROCESS

The decision-making process is all about choosing the best way to achieve goals with finite resources. There are three important points here:

- Clear goals
- Finite resources
- Choosing the best alternative

In our approach to any decision, the goal should be the starting point of our thinking. The goal is what we want to achieve with our finite resources in the end. Choosing goals—strategic decision making—is a significant decision in itself, of course.

STRATEGIC AND OPERATIONAL DECISIONS

A strategic decision is choosing the right road to run on, and an operational decision is running well on the chosen road, according to the Strategic Decisions Group. We might also describe this as choosing a goal and implementing that goal.

Strategic decisions and operational decisions cannot be separated to achieve sustained success. The action may be different and the people involved may be different for the two kinds of decision, but the decision makers must treat them as two points on a continuum in their decision-making thought process. They are interdependent for success. A good strategic decision is made to be successfully executed; a good operational decision is made to achieve the goal of the strategic decision. Every responsible strategic decision maker should regard his or her strategic decision and its execution as inseparable in a decision-making thought process; otherwise, irresponsible or non-executable decisions will be made.

Strategic decisions, which do not require frequent changes, should be made by higher-level management. Operational decisions, however, should be frequently adjusted to keep abreast of changes in the business environment. Whenever there is a better alternative for reaching the goal, adjustments should be made to operational decisions.

A WIDELY APPLICABLE DECISION FRAMEWORK

As I mentioned in the introduction, there are two common misconceptions that prevent people from adopting a common framework for all types of decision making.

The first misconception is that every decision is unique, so a general decision-making framework will not work. For instance, a decision about when to announce a new product and a decision about whom to promote from a list of competent candidates seem to be totally different. However, once you realize that all decision making is concerned with allocating finite resources to the best way of achieving the organizational goals, then you can see that the same decision-making framework can be used to consider the options and arrive at the final decisions.

The second misconception is that each decision maker is unique and cannot make decisions in the same way, because some people are rational while the others are more intuitive. Rational people rely on analyzing lots of data to make decisions and intuitive people follow their hearts—and as long as they can make good decisions, it does not matter how they make them. This misconception is based on the assumption that decision makers can know how to make good decisions repeatedly without a logical decision-making framework. It is a dangerous assumption to make.

Quality decisions require the decision makers to be both rational and innovative. A decision is not (or should not be) a one-time event, but a process of continuous improvement using the observe-think-experiment cycle. We should therefore dispel the superstition that a leader can make one good decision at a critical moment which will lead to success for a long period of time. Organizations create and sustain success when all their members make good decisions every day, and have the awareness and courage needed to adjust those decisions according to their outcome and the context.

WILLING AND ABLE—QUALITY DECISIONS

Quality decisions are made by people who *want* to make quality decisions and *know how* to make quality decisions—people who are "willing and able." An invincible team is one in which all members are willing and able.

So, a leader's role is to increase a team's willingness and ability. Willingness can be inspired through vision, mission, culture, climate, communications, and recognition systems. Ability or capability can be achieved by acquiring skills (through education, experiences, and exposure) and resources.

Of course, willing people also take the initiative to enhance their own ability; and capable people are often more willing because they are confident they know how to handle matters. So quality decision making is also a matter of "Where there's a will, there's a way"—my motto.

It takes courage to be willing, however. Ambrose Redmoon, the famous American writer, once said, "Courage is not the absence of fear, but rather the judgment that something else is more important than fear." We can have the courage to be willing to learn and try new things if we see the potential benefits; our willingness to learn then increases the odds that our decision making will be successful. While decisions always carry risk, we do not need to be afraid of that risk as long as we take on a manageable amount and consciously control it as much as possible. (Managing risk requires resources; therefore, we can only take on the risk after we have allocated resources to manage it.)

We then need to balance our courage with wisdom. I always remind myself of the Serenity Prayer: "God grant me the serenity to accept the things I cannot change; courage to change the things I can; and wisdom to tell the difference." Related to decision making, this translates as, "I must have the courage to make the best decision when it is my responsibility to allocate resources. I should also have the courage to suggest and recommend quality alternatives to other decision makers, but I need to have the serenity to accept others' final decisions when I am not the decision maker." Wisdom doesn't seem so difficult to acquire once we understand the definition of "decision."

Now that we have clarified the various terms used when discussing decision making, let's go on to look at the obstacles that can derail the decision-making process—we'll need our wisdom to deal with them.

CHAPTER 2

Decision-Making Traps

Before we get into the specifics of the GPA IPO process and how to use it, it's important to be aware of some of the obstacles to making sound decisions. Once we are aware of them, we can prevent them from affecting the decision-making process. In the book *Smart Choices* by John Hammond, Ralph Keeney, and Howard Raiffa, the authors listed many common psychological traps in decision making. In this chapter, I will describe these traps, and add three other managerial traps that I have observed.

The traps listed in *Smart Choices* are:

- the anchoring trap
- the status quo trap
- the sunk cost trap
- the confirming evidence trap
- the framing trap
- the estimating and forecasting traps of overconfidence, over-prudence and recallability.

THE ANCHORING TRAP: OVER-RELIANCE ON FIRST THOUGHTS

An anchor restricts a boat to a specific area. In the same way, our initial impressions, ideas, estimates, or other data on a certain subject often "anchor" our thoughts when making decisions. As they say, first impressions count!

One common example is when a leader expresses his or her opinion on a certain subject before the team members have had a chance to think about it on their own. This opinion from the leader often becomes an anchor that restricts the team members' range of thinking. Another example is when a beautiful actress claims that she uses ABC cosmetics and they enhance her beauty. Her testimonial has no scientific basis, yet after her fans see the endorsement, they may buy ABC's products anyway—their purchasing decision is anchored by the endorsement from this celebrity. Similarly, a spam e-mail announcing the contamination of X brand of spring water, even though it gives no proof, will deter some people from purchasing that spring water. Anchoring traps cause bias and prevent good decisions.

THE STATUS QUO TRAP: KEEPING ON KEEPING ON

People tend to maintain the status quo even if several better alternatives are available—this is the status quo trap. Inertia causes decision makers to default to the status quo and show strong prejudice against alternatives.

If the status quo is the best choice among all the alternatives, of course, that would be a quality decision. But when we stick with the status quo just because it's the status quo, without identifying other options, we may waste and misallocate our finite resources.

As I mentioned in the preface, I lived in Tokyo for seven years from 1997 to 2003. There is a passport checkpoint on the way to Narita airport (at the time of writing it is still operating), and so everyone entering the airport has to carry their passports, even if they are just going shopping at the airport or picking up their friends. Strange, right? What's the point? I asked a colleague about it, and found out that when the airport was being built in the 1960s, locals had fiercely protested against it because farmland had been confiscated for construction, and there was a lot of clamor about airport traffic. There were some violent demonstrations and protests, and so the government began to check the identities of anyone coming to the airport construction site, to prevent disturbances to the construction project. Decades later, the checkpoint is still operating even though the airport has been open for such a long time— because no one has bothered to challenge the status quo. Of course, "reasons" can always be found to maintain the status quo if the budget is still available to fund it, but those resources can certainly be used to serve better purposes in better ways. This is the status quo trap.

THE SUNK COST TRAP: PROTECTING EARLIER CHOICES

The sunk cost trap is also called the "escalation of commitment trap" or the "historical cost trap." A boat has sunk, meaning that we have lost the amount that the boat cost (the "historical" cost). The trap is to waste more money trying to salvage the sunken boat. This trap is commonly fallen into by gamblers—many will gamble more heavily after a loss, not less, in the hope of recovering the money.

Having said that, the sunk cost trap is widespread in daily life as well. Take the stock market as an example. Let's say that two months ago a group of people paid $10 per share for the stock of ABC company, and the price first rose to $13 per share, then plunged to $4 per share. Some of those stockholders will be unwilling to sell their stocks and crystallize their $6 loss, simply because the price was once $13 per share or they paid $10 per share. These people have fallen into the sunk cost trap. The historical cost of the shares has nothing to do with the decisions they have to make for the future. Since selling the stock at $13 or $10 is no longer an option, a decision needs to be made about the best way to invest the $4 each share is now worth, in order to produce the greatest future returns.

To take another example, the leaders of an organization often continue to invest money in a project that has no present value, simply because they have invested a lot of money in the project over prior years. However, if a project is not yielding a satisfactory outcome, continuing to pour money into it may not bring a better outcome. The money invested in the past cannot be recovered. The leaders should decide how the organization can generate the greatest future outcome with the resources it has in hand, and consider other, more profitable alternatives.

THE CONFIRMING EVIDENCE TRAP: SEEING WHAT YOU WANT TO SEE

The confirming evidence trap is that people tend to look for information that reinforces their argument or point of view, and steer clear of information that contradicts it.

For example, in a matrix management environment, if I wanted to promote a specific person on my team, I would tend to collect information that supported my decision. However, if my peer manager did not feel comfortable with my choice, he or she would be likely to seek information that opposed it. The confirming evidence trap affects the way we interpret information: I will give much more weight to supporting information and place little importance on conflicting ideas.

Let's go back to our Narita airport example. People can find different excuses to leave the checkpoint operating: they can say it's a good security measure or it's a passport reminder. However, if the purpose of the checkpoint is to remind people to bring their passports, surely this would be more effectively achieved by broadcasting reminders before they get on the airport coach? And it seems unlikely that the checkpoint is there for security—after all, terrorists also have passports (fake or otherwise).

THE FRAMING TRAP: POSING THE WRONG QUESTION

The framing trap is the easiest to fall into. Say you live and work in Shenzhen or New York and you receive a call from an old friend one day asking you to help her rent an apartment near your place, as she is moving to the city with her family for work. So you do your research, visit a number of apartments and recommend three to her. Afterward, you feel that you are a good friend and have been very helpful. However, you have fallen into a framing trap. You were framed by the request from your friend.

What you should have done was ask your friend whether it was appropriate to look just at apartments near your place. You should have asked what district she will be working in, how far her new workplace is from your home, and what school her children will be attending. Since you haven't taken these factors into account, the three apartments that you recommend may not be what she needs. And if she moves into one of them and find it inconvenient, she may blame you.

In an organization, the bosses may be too busy to give background information before they ask questions. Subordinates are thus often framed by their own assumptions about the questions and waste corporate resources finding the answer to a wrong question or a wrongly interpreted question. The way you ask questions affects the answer you get. In decision making, if the problem is ill-framed, it is unlikely that a good decision will be made.

ESTIMATING AND FORECASTING TRAPS

The estimating and forecasting traps are overconfidence, overprudence, and recallability. Estimation is always necessary when decisions are made about the future (remember, the future and facts are mutually exclusive). However, we often make estimations based on past experience and historical data, and if our experience was successful, we tend to be overconfident. If it was unsuccessful, we tend to be overprudent. Neither tendency will help us to make good decisions. In addition, important or dramatic events can leave a stronger impression on our memory than others, further distorting our estimates. This is the "recallability" trap.

THE THREE MOST COMMON TRAPS FOR MANAGERS

The three most common managerial decision traps I have observed in addition to the traps listed above are:

- the problem-solving trap
- the dichotomy opportunity trap
- the pass-the-buck trap.

The problem-solving trap

Usually, businesses do not make decisions to change until either 1) a problem arises, or 2) a new opportunity emerges. However, this means that they easily fall into the first two of the three common managerial decision-making traps: the problem-solving trap and the dichotomy opportunity trap.

The most prominent and prevalent trap is taking the problem as the starting point for a decision-making thought process.

Many business schools offer courses on problem solving. But while a manager's life may involve problem solving, it certainly should not be his or her main focus. Organizations hire managers because there are teams of people who need to be led and managed in order to achieve the organization's goals. Problems will inevitably arise and must be solved, but managers must not lose sight of the fact that their real mission is to lead the team to reach the goal. It is essential not to let problems be the starting point of decision making, and not to let problem solving become the goal of decision making.

Once we get onto the problem-solving track, it is difficult to change it. If we are asking the wrong question, it does not matter if we get the right answer. All the resources wasted in answering that wrong question could have been used to reach our real goal.

To put it another way, if we allow our decision-making process to start from the problem we face, we have set up a bad frame. By jumping into problem solving, we are framed by the problem, we are framed by how others have described the problem, we are framed by our seemingly limited choices, we are framed by the "urgency" of the problem, and we are framed by the limited resources we have for solving the problem. In such a situation, we usually choose the quickest, easiest solution— which could be a terrible way to reach our real goal, and could even cause more problems and prevent us from reaching our goal.

Let me give an example. One morning, a colleague of mine drove her car onto the concrete center road divider on her way to work. The car was severely damaged, but due to the car's airbag, she was not seriously hurt. She felt embarrassed as she wrote down the reason for the accident on the insurance claim form. It had been a beautiful morning with clear visibility, and she had not been drunk, or sleepy, or talking on her cell phone, or absent-minded. She had been trying to solve a problem: to stop a cup of coffee from spilling onto her dress as she came to a sharper curve than she had expected. There had been a high probability that the hot coffee would spill on her if she did not do something about it. And if it did, she would have had to give a presentation to an important client in a dress with a large coffee stain on it.

Since she did not have time to go home to change clothes, the problem was urgent, and the resources (the time available to solve the problem or change her dress) were limited. Her first thought was, "Holding the coffee is better than not holding the coffee." So she looked down and used one of her hands to keep the coffee mug steady. Taking her eyes off the road for that split second was what had caused the accident. At that moment, under those conditions, she had forgotten her primary responsibility to be a safe driver. By trying to save her coffee, she neither achieved her goal nor saved the coffee. When she gave her claim form to the insurance agent, she discovered that he frequently handled accidents caused by the very same circumstances—drivers taking their eyes off the road to attend to various situations inside the car. Many organizations become uncompetitive in the marketplace by taking their eyes off the market due to internal problems.

In some buses in Hong Kong, there is a sign above the driver that says, "Do not talk with the driver when the bus is in motion." Even if a passenger is terribly lost, the driver's responsibility is to reach each bus stop safely and in a timely manner, not to answer inquiries. The driver will thus not be considered irresponsible or unfriendly if he or she refuses to talk while driving. Losing sight of our true responsibility, for any reason, is inexcusable.

The problem-solving trap works according to the following logic of justification. When a problem occurs, we ask ourselves three questions:

1. Is this a real problem?
2. Will this problem cause real damage?
3. Is solving this problem better than not solving it?

If the answers to these three questions are all "yes," we feel justified in jumping in immediately to solve the problem. But in doing so we may totally miss the goal we want to achieve, because it was not addressed by any of the three questions.

This is a situation we face frequently in the office, isn't it? Many times we are bombarded with problems the moment we step into the office—and the problems all have to be solved, because if we don't do something about them, damage will occur. Our logic says, "Solving the problem is better than not solving the problem." Moreover, the person presenting us with the problem is generally in an urgent situation, and their urgency doesn't allow us enough time to think through the issue thoroughly. We usually don't have enough resources available to fix the problem at its root, so we use some quick and shoddy method to just get rid of it and move on—more often than not, on to the next problem. This often creates another problem down the road for ourselves or for someone else, continuing the problem-solving trap.

This logic has prevented many good managers from leading their team to achieve better performance and reach higher goals. If we spend our finite resources on solving problems, we may never achieve our current goal—sometimes, we may even forget that we have a goal. We fall into the mindset that a manager's life is solving problems.

The "problem" of budget cuts

Budget cuts are one business event that often triggers the problem-solving trap. Every company occasionally faces budget cuts, but if we solve this "problem" in the quickest way, we usually create other problems down the road.

Let me give a personal example. When I took over as IBM's vice president for marketing in the Asia-Pacific region, I looked at my budget. I was managing 14 countries, and 80 percent of the budget was given to Japan—but Japan only brought in 65 percent of the revenue. The other 13 countries had to share the remaining 20 percent of the budget, despite bringing in 35 percent of the revenue. Of course, there were historical reasons for this: when IBM established the Asia-Pacific headquarters in Japan in the 1980s, Japan was the fastest-growing country in the use of information technology. At the time, Japan contributed 80 percent of the revenue; therefore, it got 80 percent of the budget. After more than a decade, though, the market conditions had changed, and while Japan was still growing, other countries in Asia were growing faster. However, IBM's internal budgeting percentages had not changed accordingly.

I felt that this unbalanced budget was not going to help me meet the company's goal of increasing IBM's Asia-Pacific regional market share profitably. We needed to spend more resources in the faster-growing markets than in Japan's more mature market. So I knew I needed to change the budget. But that was not going to be easy. It is very difficult to change a budget distribution after the money has been received by the countries. Also, China and India were the fastest-growing markets at the time, and I am Chinese. I would be taking money from Japan to give it to China, and if I was not careful I could be accused of showing favoritism to China. So I waited for an appropriate opportunity to reallocate the budget. It came the following month, when I received an e-mail sent from the CFO to all functional VPs saying that from the next quarter we had to reduce our expenditures by 5 percent, and so we needed to resubmit our budget plans.

If I had looked at this budget cut as a problem, the best and quickest way to solve it would have been to cut 5 percent across the board from the budgets of all the countries. I could have solved the problem equitably in five seconds by forwarding the CFO's e-mail to all the marketing managers in each of my 14 countries with the message, "Please see below. Your budget will be cut 5 percent beginning next quarter. Please submit your new budget plans." That would have "solved the problem" efficiently and peacefully—and as a matter of fact, this was probably one of the reasons that the budget had gotten out of balance.

However, I saw the budget cuts as an opportunity to make each country's share more in proportion to its market potential—in order to help us achieve the goal of increasing our regional market share.

If I didn't do this right, though, I could deal Japan a devastating blow by reducing its budget so significantly. I could also destroy my relationship with Japan. And the task was particularly delicate because

I was the only female Chinese executive in the Asia-Pacific headquarters, and I was new. The marketing director for Japan and my direct boss, the Asia-Pacific general manager, were both Japanese men who had been with IBM much longer than I, and knew each other better than they knew me. Giving Japan a disproportionately large budget cut as a newly appointed VP of marketing could be a career-limiting act.

Fortunately, I had my GPA IPO framework, and using it, I helped the marketing director for Japan to see the budget cuts from a perspective beyond his own country.

To begin with, I asked him about his goals in the company. He told me that he hoped to be promoted to Asia-Pacific headquarters. Great. I offered to give him a foretaste of regional management and show him the numbers for all 14 countries. First I showed him that Japan was getting 80 percent of the budget; this made him very happy. Next I showed him that Japan only contributed 65 percent of the revenue, and asked him what he thought about that. He replied, "I didn't know that. How could this be?" No one had shown him the figures from other countries before. I explained how the budgets had got skewed over time, and asked him what he would do in my position. He was a very experienced and high-performing IBM professional, and he told me he understood what I meant. I told him that I knew budget cuts were painful and that he would have to cut programs and even let some people go. If he encountered difficulties, he could come to me and I would help him, because we were in this together.

I could not reduce Japan's share from 80 percent to 65 percent all at once. Instead, each year I reduced Japan's budget and increased some other countries' budgets to reach a more effective allocation for Asia Pacific. When I left that job after four years, Japan was receiving the marketing budget appropriate to its revenue contribution. And I had maintained good relationships with both the marketing director for Japan and my Japanese boss.

I used this approach with the rest of my team, too. I explained to them that our common goal, together with the general manager of Asia Pacific, was to grow IBM's market share in Asia Pacific, not just in Japan. I explained that we could achieve that goal through the proper allocation of our finite resources—and that to achieve the goal, we needed to reallocate those resources. This made it clear that my motivation for the changes was to achieve our common goal: I was not singling out Japan or making it a personal matter. Whether the team members emotionally liked my decision or not, they could understand my reasoning and accept my decision professionally. We were able to achieve our common goal and still maintain a good working relationship.

At this point, I would like to briefly emphasize the importance of perspective. If people cannot rise above their current role to see things from a broader perspective, from a higher-level common goal, then they will not be able to rise above their current role in the organization. It's useful to remember this when making personnel decisions.

The dichotomy opportunity trap

Problem and opportunity are two sides of the same coin—both are based on unmet needs. Unmet needs often become apparent as problems, but can also present themselves as opportunities. The second most common managerial decision trap occurs when such opportunities emerge.

The dichotomy opportunity trap is when we make a go/no-go decision with only one option on the table. There is really no choice when there is only one option.

For example, say your company wants to invest more in the emerging countries. The team for a specific emerging country brings a proposal to headquarters with a request for more resources, so you start to discuss and debate that proposal. You ask a number of questions and the team provides answers and a lot of confirming evidence that their proposal is the way to go. When it comes time to make the decision, your whole team feels, "How can we turn this down?" You have all invested in perfecting this proposal.

But at the end of the day, you only have one proposal on the table. Regardless of how good it is, you should not make a final decision with just the one proposal before you. Instead, you should have started with the company goal, which was to increase market share in emerging countries profitably. You should have sought many proposals on how to do this, and even asked the country team to submit other, significantly different proposals. Your final decision could then have included the best elements from each of the proposals—a "best of breed" solution.

So the opportunity trap works according to the following justification logic. An opportunity emerges, and we ask these questions:

1. Is this a real opportunity?
2. What are the benefits of this opportunity?
3. Do the benefits exceed the cost?

If the answers are positive, then we go after the opportunity. If not, we drop it. Either way, we have fallen into the dichotomy opportunity trap, letting a single opportunity be the starting point of our decision-making thought process. Our goal is not taken into account by the above three questions, so we allow this single opportunity to take our eyes off the original goal. A single proposal offers no choices, and without choices, there should not yet be a decision. Decision makers need to answer multiple-choice questions, not true-or-false questions.

Decision makers need to answer multiple-choice questions, not true-or-false questions

So, when making decisions, remember to avoid this trap. The time spent debating go/no-go could be better spent thinking up more ways to reach the goal. Quality decisions can only be made after multiple innovative, differentiated alternatives have been considered. A decision can never be better than the best alternative.

You can see now that both the problem-solving trap and the dichotomy opportunity trap can be avoided if we have the discipline to focus on our goal. We should not allocate our finite resources to solving a problem or pursuing an opportunity simply because it is a valid problem or a valid opportunity, but rather only if it helps us to achieve our goal. That goal should be the starting point of our decision-making thought process, and determine whether a problem is worthy of being solved or an opportunity is worthy of being pursued.

The pass-the-buck trap

The pass-the-buck trap is common in large bureaucratic organizations, where a decision may require multiple signatures from different levels of management. Line managers often generously support proposals from their own staff, with the rationale that middle or senior management can reject the proposal if it is not good enough. However, the middle manager often thinks that since a line manager already approved the proposal and senior management will inspect it again, his or her signature is not that important. So the proposal is just passed along. By the time it reaches senior management, there may be many approval signatures on it already and it may seem undemocratic to reject it. Consequently, it may be approved without anyone spending the time to really understand or inspect it. Everyone has passed the buck. No one has taken personal responsibility for the decision.

* * *

Now you know some of the most common traps in decision making, stay aware of them so that, even if you fall into one unintentionally, you don't stay there. However, don't let

The shortest route to the goal starts from the goal

avoiding traps become a false goal. Always focus on your real organizational goals. So, let's start our decision-making process from the goal, which is the topic of our next chapter. The shortest route to the goal starts from the goal.

CHAPTER 3

GPA: G for Goal

To lead a team to make the best decisions, you have to first make sure you actually have a functioning team. The two prerequisites for a working team are:

1. a shared goal
2. interdependence for success.

If you don't have these, you don't really have a team, just a group of people working together. Let's look at these two things in a little more detail.

A SHARED GOAL AND INTERDEPENDENCE FOR SUCCESS

A team goal should not only be common, objective, and outward, it should also be shared by each member subjectively and inwardly. In other words, all team members need to feel that the organizational goal matters to them personally. So, leaders need to spend a very large portion of their time communicating the goal, establishing an appropriate system for measuring progress towards it, and developing a good recognition system, so that members are motivated and willing to embrace the goal as their own.

In order for a team to be interdependent, each member of the team needs to be aware that working alone won't achieve the organization's goals—only a team can do that, due to the complexity of the tasks, the diverse skills required, and the limited time resources of individual members. However, each member also needs to be able to perform his or her job well independently, so he or she is dependable. Then, in the team as a whole, one plus one will produce more than two. Leaders who expect teamwork from their group therefore need to spend time raising team members' awareness of their interdependency and explaining that there cannot be an outcome in which one person wins while the team loses: either they all win together, or they all lose together. Of course, different members may contribute to different degrees, and different levels of recognition be given accordingly—but recognition should never be based on how team members compare with one another. If there can be individual win/loss outcomes within the team, then there will be no teamwork. Internal competition prevents teamwork and the achievement of the shared goal, as team members will focus on competing with each other instead of on the goal and on outperforming the external competitors in the marketplace. If internal competition is allowed, team members must be oriented to compete on the level of their contribution to the achievement of the shared goal.

Having said that, internal pressure on team members to perform at their best in order to maximize their contribution to the shared goal is a good thing—it promotes teamwork and helps encourage each person to become a truly dependable, high-performing team member. The key is the orientation: is the pressure orienting team members towards one another or towards achieving the shared goal? The former is a distraction to the achievement of the goal; the latter promotes teamwork and winning together. Teamwork is not the absence of conflicts: it results from the judgment that reaching the shared

Teamwork is not the absence of conflicts: it results from the judgment that reaching the shared goal is more important than conflicts

goal is more important than conflicts. Each member needs to recognize that the reason they are on the team is because they share the same goal. They are dependable members who are interdependent for success.

Goal-orientation is what differentiates effective leaders from ineffective leaders. As I said earlier, without a shared goal, the leader really does not have a team to lead. The goal is the starting point of decision-making thought process, and the destination we want to reach using our finite resources.

A shared goal must, in turn, be based on a shared positive vision of how the world could be. In the book *The Leadership Challenge*, by James M. Kouzes and Barry Z. Posner (which I highly recommend), "inspire a shared vision" is listed as one of the five practices of exemplary leadership. As the Bible says, "Where there is no vision, the people perish" (Proverbs 29:18, King James Version). The shared goal must be honorable and motivating. All members on the team should feel proud to pursue it and to be identified as a dependable member of the team.

It is worth adding here something that Henry David Thoreau, American author and historian, once said: "In the long run you only hit what you aim at. Therefore, though you should fail immediately, you had better aim at something high."

In the rest of this chapter, we'll discuss the important dimensions of a quality goal and six common failures with respect to goals. We'll finish by examining a case study that highlights some important points related to shared goals.

GOAL QUALITY

There are three important dimensions in goal quality:

1. Clear objectives
2. Defined scope
3. Conscious perspective

Clear objectives

If we know what we want to achieve, then we can allocate our resources (make a decision) to achieve our goal. I should clarify here that throughout the book, I use the word "goal" to describe what we want to achieve in the end, and "objectives" to describe one of the dimensions of the goal. Objectives are more specific and targeted, and can be shorter-term than the ultimate goal.

If we don't have a clear goal, we often find ourselves wasting resources on problem solving, as we saw in Chapter 2. And resources are finite, so there is an opportunity cost involved in all resource allocations.

Time is the most finite resource of all—everyone only has 24 hours a day, and once gone, it is gone forever. It is not renewable. Spending time on one activity entails foregoing other activities. Yes, we can multi-task, but studies have shown that our effectiveness is limited when we attend to too many different tasks concurrently.

There is a Chinese proverb that translates as, "A general should race after the goal, not after rabbits on the road" (将军赶路不赶兔). The story behind the proverb provides a good illustration of why having clear objectives is so important. Once upon a time, General A and General B went to the capital for an inauguration. General A hastened to his destination, and his galloping horse frightened the rabbits so much that they all made way voluntarily for him. By contrast, General B traveled at a leisurely pace, and the rabbits blocking his way did not scatter when they saw the horse coming. General B ended up chasing the rabbits and lost his way in the forest. Needless to say, General A got to the capital first. If General B had been asked why it took him so long to get to the capital, he would have blamed the rabbits. Yet General A would have been surprised by this answer, because he saw no rabbits on his journey.

We should not just discuss our objectives, but actively pursue them—and pursuit implies chasing with intensity. When we are chasing something, the most important thing is to keep the object in our sight: once it is out of sight, we have lost it. How often do we let our goals get out of our sight because problems come into view and distract us? As we discussed in Chapter 1, it is possible to solve all the problems that come our way and still never reach our goal, or reach the goal very slowly, like General B.

If we find too many "rabbits" blocking our way to the goal, it may mean that we have not communicated that goal clearly and frequently enough. Or maybe we are not pursuing the goal with enough intensity, and so the "rabbits" are staying on the road rather than scattering to avoid being trampled by us.

If we find ourselves busy solving problems that are unrelated to our shared goal, we need to ask ourselves these questions:

- Am I clear about the goal?
- Are the people around me clear about the goal?
- Am I furiously pursuing the goal?
- Are people bringing me problems that are unrelated to the goal because they are not clear about the goal?
- Have they heard me communicating what the goal is?
- Do they realize I am serious about this goal?
- Do they think I have additional resources (including time resources) to spend on pursuits that are unrelated to this goal?
- Am I helping others to be clear about the goal?

We may need to adjust both our communication and our pursuit so that the people around us will automatically "give way" or join us in pursuing the shared goal.

Goals also need to be grounded in a long-term dream. How long is long enough? Well, once I asked my MBA students how long-range their life goals were, and some answered, "One year." That answer would only have been acceptable if they intended to live for just one more year! If they'd hoped to live for another, say, 80 years, a one-year goal could cause them to make decisions that might negatively impact their remaining 79 years of life. Our long-term goals should match the potential total resources we will have in the long run. So a life goal should match the potential "time resources" we will have in life—"long-range" means "lifetime" in this case.

Unlike a person, of course, an organization is a legal entity, and should be able to live forever if its decision makers constantly make quality decisions. So, all our decisions within an organization should have a very long-term perspective, even if the scope of each decision may be restricted by the available resources at the time. If an organization does not have a long-term goal, it will be aimless once the short-term goal is reached.

Organizations often define their long-term goals using vision and mission statements. Vision and mission statements are not lip service, but the most important starting point of quality managerial decisions. They are the basis for the more specific shared objectives developed by the organization's divisions, departments, and functional groups. These sub-level goals and objectives comprise different ways to contribute to the achievement of the company vision and mission.

The vision statement describes the future state the organization desires to bring about; the desirable picture it paints is intended to motivate all team members to make the shared dream come true. The mission statement answers the questions, "Why does the world need this organization?", "What does the world gain by having this organization?", and "What will the world lose without this organization?" If the world would not miss the organization if it did not exist, then sooner or later it will not exist. Hence, the ultimate goal of any organization (and individual, come to that) is to create value for the world. Every organization creates its value in different ways, but it must create it for some people, somewhere, somehow, in order to continue to exist.

A good vision statement helps all members to visualize the desired future state, which can then become the motivating force for all managerial actions. A good mission statement gives meaning to the daily activities of all members. "An effective mission statement balances the possible with the impossible" according to Jack Welch. Quality vision and mission statements make all members proud of representing the organization—if they are practiced and lived out in every managerial decision.

Defined scope

An attainable goal in decision making needs to have a defined scope. Many people have the goal of being the best in their country and then the best in the world. This is a motivating dream, but it is not practical enough to use when leading a team to make day-to-day decisions. "Being the best" can be defined differently in different contexts; for example, do you mean you want to be number one in sales revenue, gross profits or profit margin? Number one in brand value? Number one in customer satisfaction? Number one in market share? "The best" needs to be defined in order for us to be able to allocate our resources in its pursuit. And if we have multiple goals—e.g. profit and market share—we need to assign them a different priority, stage by stage.

One of my students was working in the children's clothing industry, and told me his goal for his company was to become the number-one children's clothing company in the world. This is a wonderful dream. But a dream needs a defined scope to become an attainable goal that we can base decision making on. What did his dream include and exclude at this stage? Did "children's clothing" encompass both swaddling for newborn babies and clothes for 12-year-old boys and girls? Were underwear, pajamas, school uniforms and formal attire all included? Were high-end, middle-end and low-end markets included? Without a defined scope, the student's dream will never become an attainable goal, due to his lack of focus on allocating his finite resources.

Also, we need to know what our time frame is for our goal. A year, five years, 10 years? And how long do we want to sustain this position? Our goals can only be turned into reality if we define them well.

Conscious perspective

Each decision also requires a conscious perspective. In other words, *in whose view* do you want to be "number one in children's clothing"? Are you putting yourself in the children's shoes, the parents' shoes, investors' shoes, employees' shoes, society's shoes, or distributors' shoes? All these different parties will have different perspectives on the matter. The children's first choice of clothing brand may be very different from the choice of their parents; the number-one choice from the shareholders' perspective may be different from the best choice from the employees' perspective.

With finite resources, it's not possible to satisfy all parties' needs equally at the same time. It's also impossible to compete with every company in your field in the world. So, you must define your perspective.

* * *

To sum up, we need to have a clear long-term vision, under which shorter-term objectives should be established. We also need to have a defined scope for each decision, indicating what to include and exclude and for how long a time this decision holds true. All companies want to be the market leader, and may even share the same mission and vision; however, their defined scopes and perspectives will differ greatly and result in very different decisions generating very different outcomes.

A long-term goal should not be achievable in one step; if it is, we are not reaching high enough. As we attain each shorter-term objective successfully, we will gain additional resources to continue the journey toward our long-term goal. Step by step, we'll progress toward it, as long as we do not lose sight of it while we're pursuing our shorter-term objectives—and as long as those shorter-term objectives have been set in such a way that they will lead to the realization of the long-term goal.

To go back to the children's clothing example: say my student was to decide that, while his long-term dream is still to be number one in the world, his shorter-term strategy is to target children below the age of six, and that he will position his clothing range as high-end product with a higher profit margin. He would be aiming to be number one in profit and brand value. This means he should not try to solve the problem of some customers complaining that his products are too high-priced or don't fit nine-year-olds, because the defined scope of his goal is "below age six," "brand value," and "profit." He can focus his finite resources on achieving that goal. Once it has been achieved, he should have gained more resources, allowing him to expand his customer segments to cover a wider age span, wider product offerings, or wider geographies.

COMMUNICATING THE GOAL

Organizational goals must be openly and frequently communicated to share them among all members of the team. Remember, a shared goal and interdependence to succeed are the two prerequisites for a team. If these two conditions have not been met, we may have got a group of people together, but we don't really have a team. So we don't really need teamwork, even though we may want to have it to make life more pleasant. Teamwork is needed only when all members share the same goal and are interdependent for success. That means each member takes the organizational goal as his or her own professional goal, and each is a dependable member of the team.

It's especially important, when communicating the team goal, that the leader's personal goal is not in conflict with it. If conflict exists, sooner or later the leader will face a situation in which he or she must choose between personal and organizational goals. This is a no-win position, and the leader's credibility is jeopardized as the team members become skeptical about the conflict of interest.

As a leader, ask yourself the following question: "If I had to make my personal goals public, could I do it?" The answer should be yes. If the answer is no—why not? What is there to hide? Leadership is a role, and responsibilities come with that role. We must not put ourselves in a position where personal and organizational goals must be traded off. The two must be aligned and interdependent for us to succeed.

COMMON FAILURES REGARDING GOALS

There are six common failures with respect to goals:

1. We often plunge too deeply into problems, as mentioned earlier—focusing on solving those problems and forgetting about our goals. The goal we want to achieve should always be our starting point for decisions, not problems. History cannot be changed, but the future is made by our decisions. All decisions are about the future, so unless we start with the future in mind, we will have no future.

   Unless we start with the future in mind, we will have no future

2. We confuse the means and the ends, insisting on using certain methods of achieving our goals while compromising the goals themselves. Managers often make the mistake of being dictatorial about *how* the shared goal should be achieved, and use this to divide the team into "those who are on my side" and "those who are not," instead of allowing the shared goal to unite the team members and inspire them to find different,

innovative ways of achieving it. All dictators have visions and goals, but insist on only using their own means to reach those goals. Managers who dictate methods waste the multifarious talents of the team and limit innovation and creativity.

3. We try to make our goals very innovative, when it is the means of achieving them that should be innovative. Goals can be very basic—for example, peace and happiness have been humanity's goals through all of human history, and sustainable success has always been the main corporate goal. These goals don't have to be changed because they're not new or "fancy." The means to achieve these goals, however, should certainly change according to time and situation. Innovation is definitely needed in this area.

4. Our goals are not sufficiently high or long-range. If our goals are too easily achievable and too short term, we will frequently be aimless.

5. There is a conflict of interest between the leader's personal goals and team goals. As we mentioned earlier, in this case, the leader's hidden agenda will reduce the quality of the decisions made.

6. The team members have different unstated assumptions about the future. All our decisions are based on our assumptions and predictions of what will happen in the future, and these assumptions may be proven right or wrong in the future due to various reasons which may not be controllable by us. So, when making goals, we need to communicate clearly what assumptions were made about the future, so that we can explicitly measure these assumptions and make timely adjustments in the future.

The ultimate goal for every organization is to create value. Due to our finite resources, however, we cannot equally satisfy every need at the same time with each decision. This is why we need to prioritize—which is the P in our GPA acronym. However, before we move on to Chapter 4 to discuss this, let's look at a case study that will help us better understand the importance of a shared goal as the starting point of our decision-making process.

CASE STUDY

All the case studies in this book have been taken, with slight modifications, from *Case Studies in International Management* by Christopher Sawyer-Laucanno. We thank Pearson Education for their permission to use them.*

We have chosen cases from the book that represent different geographies, cultures, industries, management levels, roles, and types of decisions, in order to illustrate that the GPA IPO decision-making framework can be used for all kinds of decisions. The cases simulate real-life situations.

The situation: Millars Bank Ltd.

Mr. P. D. Smothers, manager of Millars Bank Ltd. in Abu Dhabi, the United Arab Emirates, paced the floor of his stately office. Looking out through the large window across the busy modern city, he contemplated his next move regarding his newly arrived corporate loan officer, J. L. Marsh. *Ms. J. L. Marsh.*

Ms. Marsh had come highly recommended. She had been in corporate banking for 12 years, the last 10 of which had been spent in Beirut and Cairo. Ms. Marsh spoke Arabic fluently, and had been credited with arranging a number of highly complex yet extremely successful loans in her former position.

But last week she had been assigned to his office, and in the United Arab Emirates women did not hold such positions.

Smothers had at first been delighted. The previous loan officer, a British gentleman, had moved to a more suitable job at headquarters, and there was no local candidate who was qualified to take over the position. The head office in England had telexed the news that it had found a suitable replacement, and had included a brief account of Ms. Marsh, an account that surpassed his expectations. But, in typical telex fashion, the head

---

* Excerpts pp. 28–30, 40–42, 55–57, 82–84, 93–97 from CASE STUDIES IN INTERNATIONAL MANAGEMENT by Christopher Sawyer-Laucanno. Copyright © 1987 by Prentice-Hall, Inc. Reprinted by permission of Pearson Education, Inc.

office had only used initials: J. L. Marsh. The last thing he had expected was that J. L. would turn out to stand for "Janet Louise."

Dialogue: The right person for the job?

Characters: P.D. Smothers, Bank Manager, Millars Bank, Abu Dhabi
Janet Marsh, New Loan Officer, Millars Bank, Abu Dhabi

Mr. Smothers and Ms. Marsh meet in Mr. Smothers' office in Abu Dhabi.

Smothers: Miss Marsh, I frankly don't know what to say. I would have thought, with your obvious knowledge of the Middle East, that you would have disqualified yourself from this position.

Marsh: Mr. Smothers, I understand what you're trying to tell me, but I really don't see that we have a problem. Believe it or not, when I was first transferred to Cairo five years ago, John, John Phillips, the manager there, had very much the same reservations you have today.

Smothers: I know John. Know him very well.

Marsh: Well, it worked out beautifully.

Smothers: But Egypt is not Abu Dhabi. Egypt is progressive, very liberal, women are acknowledged as professionals. But in the Emirates . . .

Marsh: You don't want me to stay.

Smothers: It's not me. Please understand that. I would be delighted to have you stay. But, but, I can't imagine, Miss Marsh, how you could do your job. Our clients are conservative, traditional. They expect their principal loan officer to be a man. They won't do business with us. They won't take us seriously.

Marsh: Why not?

Smothers: They just won't. It's simply not done. Unheard of, even.

Marsh: With all due respect, I think you're vastly mistaken.

Smothers: What?

Marsh: That's right. Mistaken. Our clients come to our bank to borrow pounds in order to finance projects that must be paid in pounds. Nothing more, nothing less. What they are looking for is a loan officer who can place their loan at a competitive interest rate and in short order. Isn't that correct?

Smothers: Yes. And no.

Marsh: Why no?

Smothers: Miss Marsh, you've been in corporate banking long enough to realize that personal relations between a client and a lending institution are vitally important. I, I can't see how our clients could, would relate to you. And we're not the only bank in town, either. Why, just in Abu Dhabi alone there are at least two dozen foreign banks with whom we are in direct competition, not to mention the other two dozen Emirate-owned banks, plus all the other foreign banks with representatives on restricted licenses who can take business away from us.

Marsh: Mr. Smothers, I am well aware of the competition and the role of the loan officer. I am so well aware, in fact, that I feel that I can be as effective or more effective here than I was in Beirut and Cairo. I understand the Middle East. I've lived here for many years. I speak, read, and write Arabic. I know the customs, the religion, the history, and, most importantly, the business of business. How many other loan officers are fluent in Arabic?

Smothers: Not many. I'm not even myself. But that has not been a disadvantage.

Marsh: Has it been an advantage?

Smothers: No, I can't say that either.

Marsh: Besides, Mr. Smothers, let me remind you that this is a British bank, not an Arab bank and—

Smothers: But a British bank in an Arab country.

Discussion

In this situation, there were two main reasons that Mr. Smothers and Ms. Marsh could not reach a common decision.

First, Mr. Smothers started his decision-making process from the problem instead of from their shared goal. This case study is set in the 1980s, but even today, in many countries, attitudes to gender roles are a difficult cultural problem to solve swiftly. If we start with the problem, we quickly come to the conclusion that the challenge is too big, and that it is not the role of a bank to change the entire national culture. So, to Mr. Smothers, it seems that the best solution is not to have a female loan officer, regardless of Ms. Marsh's competence and willingness. Maintaining the status quo will be the safest choice.

Second, Mr. Smothers and Ms. Marsh made different assumptions about the future based on their different experiences in the past. Mr. Smothers assumed that customers would not accept a female British loan officer because they had never worked with a female loan officer in the past. He assumed that the future would most probably be the same as the past. On the other hand, Ms. Marsh assumed that she could perform well in the new job because of her successful past experiences in other Arab countries; again, she assumed that the future would most probably be the same as her past.

So, whose assumption about the future is correct? No one can tell at this stage—remember, the future offers no facts. However, one thing we do know is that unless we try new things and experiment, we will never find out whose assumption is correct. If we start our decision from a problem, we will not be able to make any team decision effectively, and in the end we will probably neither solve the problem (here, cultural biases regarding gender) nor achieve the goal (better business performance for the loan department). If we start our decision-making process from the shared goal, by contrast, we can work out innovative ways to achieve the goal while managing risk together.

There are always risks involved in experiments, but without them we will never make progress. So, the focus for Mr. Smothers and Ms. Marsh should be their shared goal (increasing the revenue and profits of the bank) and how they can minimize and manage the risks together. If the risks are manageable, they can experiment. Also, they should make a backup plan in case the risk increases in the future.

They then need to reach a mutual understanding on how to measure their progress toward success, since this is an experiment. With that measurement system in place, they can make timely adjustments as needed. If they can manage the risks and reach their shared goal together, the seemingly unsolvable "cultural bias regarding gender" problem will be solved during the process. However, if Mr. Smothers remains focused on the problem, he will never solve it, only skirt around it and waste a valuable employee. If the risks increase, he can trigger the backup plan. Furthermore, there will be no bad feelings between them because they shared the same goal and worked interdependently for success.

This case demonstrates both the need for a shared goal in business teamwork and the importance of making that shared goal the starting point of managerial decisions, rather than problems. It also illustrates the status quo trap (Mr. Smothers) and the overconfidence trap (Ms. Marsh), and reminds us that while we cannot universally apply past experiences to the unknown future, we can learn lessons from the past that can help us generate alternative methods of reaching a goal. In addition, because each situation does contain a certain element of risk, we need to build risk management into our action plans—this will be discussed in Chapter 6.

So, now that we have seen why we should start every decision at our shared goal, we can move on to a discussion of the next component in our GPA framework: Priorities.

CHAPTER 4

GPA: P for Priorities

After setting a long-term goal, we have to identify the most important thing to do next to achieve it. Because our resources are finite, we cannot do everything at the same time, so we have to set short-term and mid-term priorities. Without a clear goal, there is no way to prioritize, because prioritizing means closing the gap between the current state and our future desired state. Without a clear goal, we will not even know what the gap to close is! Prioritization is where real trade-offs are made, so it is the most difficult element in the decision-making process. Once a long-term goal is chosen, it does not need to be changed often, but priorities can change dramatically depending on what the gaps are between the current state and the goal.

Whenever we have multiple choices (e.g. multiple alternatives or multiple objectives) and insufficient resources to achieve them all at the same time, we need to prioritize. Having multiple objectives is very common—most companies, for example, have a group of objectives like customer satisfaction, employee morale, profitability, market share, product quality, and brand value. We have to prioritize these objectives by either giving them a different timing or a different weight when it comes to resource allocation. There are four Chinese words that express this nicely— 轻重缓急, "light/heavy, slow/fast," meaning that you cannot treat everything equally. This explains the essence of priority (优先级). Treating everything as equally important and equally urgent is not a winning strategy, and it often causes confusion and frustration internally. Priorities should also be different at different stages of the product life cycle, just as people should have different priorities at different stages of life.

We need to prioritize our alternatives, too, since we should consider multiple alternatives before making final decisions. Not all alternatives are equal in terms of importance, impact, efficiency, and effectiveness. In short, whenever there are multiple objectives or alternatives, we need to prioritize, and use our finite resources first on the most important objective and the best alternative.

WHAT IS A PRIORITY?

President John F. Kennedy gave a good definition of priority in his speech at Rice University on September 12, 1962, when he announced to the nation that he would make the space project a national priority and that the USA would put a man on the moon before the end of the 1960s. His speech explained that priority means a "challenge . . . we are willing to accept, one that we are unwilling to postpone, and one which we intend to win . . . we must pay what needs to be paid . . . in spite of uncertainties and unknowns, we must be bold."

We face many challenges every day; if we accept all of them, we could end up achieving nothing. To prioritize is to choose the challenges that we are willing to accept, intend to win and plan to pay what is necessary to achieve properly and successfully.

HOW ARE PRIORITIES SET?
Having a baseline

Prioritization is not easy, because we tend to want it all now, and are reluctant to label anything "not important" in case it becomes very important later. Prioritizing is not, however, about whether certain matters are important or not, but about which matter is *more* important *now*. So leaders and managers should clarify priorities after the long-term goal has been communicated.

Priorities can and should change with time, and they can be different in different contexts. However, there should be a clear baseline that can never be crossed at any time. This

> There should be a clear baseline that can never be crossed at any time

could be externally driven, for example, paying taxes and meeting other legal obligations; or internally directed, such as commitment to customers, company credibility, personal integrity, and corporate values. These baseline items must be absolutely protected with the resources available, with no trade-offs considered. Resources must be allocated *first* to cover these baseline items. Otherwise, they are not really baseline to us, and they will be exposed sooner or later. Baseline matters give us the solid foundation for sustained success; without them, the company cannot sustain its existence—or it will not be worth sustaining. Companies that have failed miserably did not do so because they did not reach their higher goals, but because they did not cover their baseline first, or did not have a baseline.

Baseline items, once established, are never negotiable, and it is the responsibility of leaders and managers to communicate this to all employees. Some companies put them into a written "code of conduct" and have employees sign to certify that they have read the code and have agreed to comply with it. However, managers cannot assume that all employees will automatically know and understand these baseline items. They also cannot assume that the baseline will be protected unless specific resources are actively allocated to protect it—resources such as education and training, and compliance audits.

Although we are goal-driven, we cannot use any and all means to pursue our goals. Any means that are below the baseline can never be considered. We should be innovative in coming up with means that are above the baseline.

Performance gap or opportunity gap?

Since the long-term goal is our future desired state, not the current state, there will be many gaps between the two states. We should analyze and prioritize the gaps, and then allocate resources to close the most important gap first.

In their book *Winning Through Innovation*, Michael L. Tushman and Charles A. O'Reilly identify two types of gaps that usually exist in business: performance gaps and opportunity gaps. Companies win in the marketplace only when outstanding performance meets opportunity. Hence, we can analyze the gaps between our current state and the future desired state by asking, "Do we have a performance gap or an opportunity gap? Are we missing competitive capabilities or are we missing opportunities to compete?" While a performance gap can usually be closed by improving capability and execution, an opportunity gap must usually be closed by a change in business model. Both gaps can be closed by resource allocation, but we must know which to close in order to be able to use our finite resources to produce an optimal outcome. The gaps will change over time, and will differ according to the market conditions. But it is only when we have outstanding capabilities coupled with the opportunity to show and use them that we will win in the marketplace. And to sustain that success, we must continue allocating our resources to enhance performance and generate opportunities.

Important, not urgent

If we always do the most important thing first, there will usually be very few urgent matters to handle

When setting priorities, we should always consider importance first, not urgency. If we always do the most important thing first, there will usually be very few urgent matters to handle. Most urgent internal matters are self-inflicted, due either to a lack of proper planning or a lack of constant monitoring of changes in the environment. Very few urgent matters are truly "unforeseeable."

If we maintain a continuous improvement cycle of observe-think-experiment, then all action should be considered an experiment;

otherwise, we are not innovating. Progress toward the goal should be measured, so that we can observe again, think again, and act again with improvements. If our actions cannot be called experiments, it means that we are maintaining the status quo. We are doing what we have done before; we are not trying new ideas, new ways of doing things. If our action can, however, be called an experiment, then success is not guaranteed, so we must measure our progress, make timely adjustments and improve again. But our plans should lead the changes, instead of letting "urgent" matters chase us around and chase our goal out of sight. We must train ourselves to always do the most important thing first—and that is to close the most relevant gaps between the current state and our long-term goal.

Some gaps have dependencies and sequences which cannot be ignored or skipped. In these situations, we can prioritize according to this sequence of events, first things first. For example, we must have a competitive product to offer the market before we spend any resources to establish the distribution network for delivering that product or engaging in any promotional activities.

We take risks in good managerial practice, but that does not mean we gamble carelessly, it means that we dare to experiment with good risk management procedures in place. Innovation is a discipline we should learn to practice. Good managerial practice increases our odds of winning through continuous improvement.

Matters of equal importance

If there are several matters of equal importance before us, we should assess their degrees of positive impact and risk in order to set priorities. Many matters seem to be of equal importance but have different degrees of impact: we should prioritize the matter that will generate the most positive impact first, because our resources will achieve a greater positive outcome. If the impacts are also similar, we should prioritize the task with fewer difficulties or less risk.

If there are several things with similar importance and similar impact and risk, we can prioritize them by the size of their window of opportunity. The narrower the window of opportunity, the higher the priority. However, we only need to consider this *after* we have made sure the matter is truly important enough to pursue in light of our goal. Windows of opportunity mean nothing if they are not for important matters to begin with! Again, we need to resist any sense of urgency imposed on us by other people's poor planning.

Importance is relative

So, priorities are "the most important things"—but importance is relative. We need to ask, "Is there anything more important?" and "What is the most important thing?" This is the most difficult part of the GPA IPO framework.

Let me give you an example. When managing the annual marketing budget at IBM, I would set aside a discretionary fund in my budget to meet unanticipated expenses during the year. It was not meant to compensate for poor planning, but to address those things that come up in the marketplace unexpectedly, that we do not have any way of foreseeing. I explained this to the country marketing managers on the team.

One year, the manager from a small country came to me and applied for US$30,000 from this discretionary fund. I said, "Okay, let's talk about what you want to do with the money." He told me that he had just been notified that an international industry conference was going to be held in the capital city of his country that year. The conference organizers had given him one month to decide if his team would participate: they would need US$30,000 to pay for their booth and make the exhibit.

I said, "Since this is a resource allocation, let's talk about the goal, the priorities, and the alternatives." With respect to our goal, the manager explained the importance of this conference, its large size, and how many important worldwide decision makers would attend. He went on to say that IBM should be at the conference to show that it cares about this market segment and to take advantage of the visibility that the conference afforded. He also told me attending the conference would boost the IBM brand and generate sales leads.

"Okay," I said. "So as far as the goal is concerned, you want to enhance the IBM brand and generate leads for sales. I've got that. But now let's talk about priorities. Is an IBM booth at this international conference the most important thing to do to close the gap between your current state and the goal you just stated? Let's say I gave this US$30,000 to you, but said it was the only additional budget that you could get from the discretionary fund for the rest of the year, even if something else unexpected happened in the market. Is there something more important than this three-day event that you could spend the money on to reach those goals this year? Please think about this, discuss it with your team, and come back in a week with your answer."

When he came back to see me, he started by saying, "I want to be absolutely sure I understand. You said that you will give me the money; you wanted me to work on the most important thing; and the US$30,000 is the only additional resource that you will give me this year." I said, "Well, that was not quite the way I put it. However, I can now decide to give you the funds, but I want to ensure you work on the most important thing first. So what is your answer?" He said, "Thank you very much for the money. After discussion, our team decided that we would use an additional US$30,000 to hire a telemarketing contractor to do telesales for us for the whole year. This will provide us with a much higher return than attending the conference."

I liked his answer, as I agreed that this was a better way to spend the budget to reach the business goal. Still, I asked, "What about the event? You said it was so important for IBM to be there." He said, "Yes, it is very important. As a matter of fact, it is so important that IBM should not ask our small country to fund attendance, because it is an annual event, and we can only do it for this one year. IBM should not be there one year and skip the next. Also, the leads generated from this event will go to countries all over the world. So I think that the money required to attend this event should come from Asia-Pacific headquarters or even from the worldwide headquarters. Actually, I think worldwide headquarters should consider participating in the event every year."

I also liked this answer, because if it was truly such an important event, then IBM should spend the resources to be there every year, no matter which country was hosting it, and allocate funds from headquarters to do so.

You can see how effective this approach was. This manager changed his own mind. He didn't think, "Okay, because last time I said that this conference was the most important thing, this time I have to say the same thing." The premise had changed: the first time he came to me, he did not have the US$30,000, so of course he said that the conference was important in order to get the money. Once he was assured he could have the money, the assumptions changed, and so the answer should also change.

Also, he and his team found a better way to achieve the goal, by using a telemarketing contractor—a better use of resources for such a small country. So, he was willing to change his previous decision when he found out that his previous assumption was now invalid and a better alternative had emerged. Of course, one should never do this as a staged "plot" to get more budget, or to get the budget for one reason and use it on some other item. I know this was an honest change, because he had no idea how I was going to respond to his original request. And the one-year telemarketing contract gave him the flexibility to continue or not at the end of the year.

He had also showed that he knew how to leverage other people's resources. Using his small office's resources to attend a large international conference was not the wisest decision, so he recommended that the Asia-Pacific or worldwide headquarters consider spending the resources for IBM to attend this conference consistently every year—if it was truly important to the corporation.

He had done an excellent job of prioritizing. I told him, "Okay, you may have the US$30,000, and if during the year some other truly unexpected market conditions arise, do feel free to come and apply for funds from the discretionary fund again." But he didn't come back that year. He used his resources very wisely, he met his goal very effectively for that year, and eventually, I promoted him to a regional position.

I think this example shows us clearly how prioritization works. It is not just a true and false question, "Is this good to do?" It is a matter of deciding what the one right thing is for us to do among many things, and of deciding how we can best use our finite resources to reach our goal.

To sum up, here are some helpful hints about setting priorities:

- Cover the compulsory items such as legal compliance.
- Cover the baseline that cannot be crossed, whatever that may be for you (a commitment to customers and corporate value, for example).

- Examine the gaps between your current state and your long-term goal, and prioritize them according to their importance for achieving the goal. Close the most important gap first.

- Analyze the sequence of events and do the first thing first (e.g. create a competitive product before starting promotional activities).

- Understand the degree of impact that each matter will have, and prioritize whatever will have the highest positive impact.

- Establish the degree of risk and uncertainty. If several matters are equally important, or will have an equally positive impact, then prioritize the matter with lowest risk or uncertainty first.

- If several matters are equally important, will have equal impacts, and have equal risks, then prioritize the matter with the shortest window of opportunity.

COMMON FAILURES IN SETTING PRIORITIES

Usually, if we find setting priorities to be daunting, it means our goal is not clear enough or not long-term enough. Clear, truly long-term goals should make prioritization easier, not harder. If the most important thing to do next is also our ultimate goal, however, then we are really aimless. We are too shortsighted, and we will soon either be without a goal, when our short-term goal is achieved, or we will have failed utterly, if we did not achieve our short-term goal and have no other goals to pursue. The Chinese proverb, "Failure breeds success" (失败为成功之母), only applies to people who have proper long-term goals—in this situation, a failure is a good lesson learned along the way to success. But without a long-term goal, any failure will be total and ultimate, since you have nothing to look to beyond it.

The common failures in priority setting are:

- assuming the baseline is covered automatically, without explicitly allocating adequate resources to it
- treating everything as equally important—not being willing to deselect or de-prioritize anything

- confusing the urgent with the important
- not being able to distinguish "impact" from "importance"
- ignoring the important intangibles or "indirect" values because they are not easily quantifiable and not urgent (e.g. not allocating resources to promote the brand itself, as distinct from promoting a specific product)
- having insufficient clarity on trade-offs
- ignoring dependencies
- ignoring time value and windows of opportunity
- spending most of your finite resources to solve problems created in the past, instead of using them to close the gap between the current state and the future goal.

* * *

To sum up, there are four questions that will help us to test whether we have our priorities right. They are:

1. What is the baseline that cannot be traded off?
2. What is the most important gap to close between the current state and our future goal?
3. If this were my last additional resource, how could I best spend it to achieve my goal?
4. Among all the important matters, which one has the narrowest window of opportunity?

Now, let's go on to look at a case study in priorities.

CASE STUDY

The situation: The Tanaka Komuten Company

The Tanaka Komuten Company is a large Japanese general contractor noted for its excellence in the design and construction of offices, commercial and public buildings, multi-family housing, schools, and hotels.

This family-owned company has grown rapidly since its founding in the 1950s, attaining a position as one of the top five construction firms in Japan. This success, in the opinion of the Tanaka family, is attributable to one main factor: the non-diversified character of the company.

The strategy of specialization has proved quite effective during the last decades. The company easily gained building contracts, most of which were sole-sourced due to its excellent reputation and track record, and won numerous awards for its high-quality construction. In recent years, however, there has been a decline in building construction in Japan, and the Tanaka Komuten Company found itself, for the first time, in a rather precarious position.

It is clear that the old course of specialization is no longer as tenable as it has been. What direction the company should pursue now, though, is a matter of internal controversy. The chairman of the board, Mr. Kazuo Tanaka, and his son, the president, Mr. Ruichi Tanaka, are resisting expanding the firm into other areas of construction. They have serious doubts as to whether they can compete with more established firms in other areas, and fear that a move toward diversification will damage their reputation for excellence.

Most of the directors feel that the company should expand its civil engineering capacity, which accounts for less than 4 percent of its total sales. However, the Tanakas are resisting this idea as well, saying that this would drain away too many resources from the main business activity and, again, possibly affect their reputation. After months of discussion without any resolution, the position of the directors is strengthened by a new development: An offer is received from a former US construction partner, Atlas Engineering & Construction, to form a joint venture company for the purpose of international civil engineering and building construction.

Dialogue: A joint venture consideration

Characters: Tom Jameson, President, Atlas Engineering & Construction
Kenji Taniguchi, Managing Director, Tanaka Komuten
Kazuo Tanaka, Chairman, Tanaka Komuten
Ruichi Tanaka, President, Tanaka Komuten

In the Osaka head office of Tanaka Komuten, the American and Japanese executives are discussing the possibilities of forming a joint venture company.

Jameson: By now I'm sure you've had a chance to look over some of the documents I sent from Houston. I think it should be fairly clear that a joint venture for the purpose of obtaining world-wide contracts involving both civil and building engineering would be advantageous for both of us.

K. Tanaka: There certainly are some positive aspects to your proposal. We still have some concerns, though.

Jameson: Of course. A number of details need to be ironed out, even explored further. What is your main concern?

K. Tanaka: Our main concern, to be perfectly honest, has little to do with the proposal itself. In fact, we find it rather sound. The problem is simply this: Tanaka Komuten has built a reputation on its commitment to design and building construction. We pride ourselves on this. It's what makes us different from our competitors.

Taniguchi: Yes. This policy is at the core of our business philosophy.

Jameson: I understand that. The fact of the matter, though, is this: By combining our respective strengths, we are not diminishing our own primary commitment either to building or civil engineering.

Taniguchi: In one way, that's true. In another, it isn't. By forming a separate company, we do maintain our primary enterprise as is. On the other hand, a major resource commitment, both in capital and in manpower, cannot help but affect Tanaka Komuten as a general contractor.

Jameson: But as I see it, we are already committed to that course. When we worked together on the past project, with you building the terminal and us the runways, we were doing just that. Also, I don't see that Tanaka Komuten will be changing its emphasis at all. You will still be in charge of design and building construction, and Atlas in charge of civil engineering. What our joint venture company would do is simply make it easier to bid on projects. Currently, there are two international projects for us to pursue, one in Singapore, one in

Brazil. A joint venture between us will increase the odds of winning for both of us.

R. Tanaka: That's a good point. It would definitely make it easier for prospective clients as well. The problem, though, is with our image. Will our existing clients see it that way, or will they feel that Tanaka Komuten has gone the way of all major contractors?

Jameson: If we make our relationship clear, do a little public relations work, I don't see any problem.

Taniguchi: It definitely bears consideration. There's obviously a lot to gain from a joint venture.

Jameson: And little risk, really. Also, since we will not do any joint venture work in Japan, your domestic clients will not be at all affected. And let's face it; we need each other if we are to start increasing our growth. There are a lot of international revenue opportunities, and with our collective experience and reputations I really think we can turn this joint venture into a very profitable partnership.

At this point, Jameson presented some confirming evidence to the Tanakas about forming the joint venture.

Following is an excerpt from the proposal to Tanaka Komuten which summarizes its main points.

Joint venture proposal to Tanaka Komuten

Main activities of the joint venture company: To procure contracts internationally for projects involving both civil engineering and building construction; e.g. the design and construction of transportation facilities, rural factories requiring road and rail extensions, urban and regional planning and development, harbor facilities. In addition, the joint venture company would engage in activities related to these projects, such as material procurement, construction design and engineering (both civil and building), structural engineering, and land-use planning.

Purpose of the joint venture: To consolidate civil engineering and building construction capabilities in one single corporation. The immediate advantages of such a consolidation are:

1. Elimination of separate bid submission, thus reducing the cost factor involved in international feasibility study preparation.
2. Assurance to the client of integrated design, engineering, construction, and quality control.
3. Reduction in overall costs to the client.
4. Placement of Tanaka Komuten and Atlas Engineering in a competitive position in relation to other consolidated engineering and construction firms.

Investment capital: Subject to negotiation and eventual scope of business. Probable minimum investment is US$5 million each.

Equity: Equal participation, hence equal equity.

Distribution of profit and loss: Subject to negotiation and eventual structure of the joint venture company. On most projects, however, equal sharing is desirable. On some projects requiring additional resources to be provided by the respective parent companies, a percentage of invested capital, materials, and manpower resources will be returned/borne by the parent company.

Immediate prospects for joint venture bids:

- Singapore—Marina City, apartments and roads
- Brazil—Porto Alegre–Sao Paulo, rail and terminal improvements

Discussion

When I asked my MBA students to make a decision about whether Tanaka Komuten should agree to the joint venture, most of them immediately tried to get more information on Atlas, Tanaka Komuten, and the Singapore and Brazil international bidding opportunities. Their decision-making process then focused on:

- the strengths and weaknesses of Atlas and Tanaka Komuten
- the cost and benefits of a joint venture with Atlas

- the joint venture terms and conditions (e.g. the share percentage, management and control, the name and PR, whether to pursue both the Singapore and Brazil opportunities, risks, and how to partner).

After discussion, most of my students chose to collaborate with Atlas either through the proposed joint venture or through a joint bid of some sort.

When I asked them how many choices they had, some said two: a joint venture with Atlas or not. Some said many: a joint venture with Atlas, a joint bid with Atlas without forming a joint venture, a joint venture with Atlas with a majority share, a joint venture with Atlas with a minority share, and so on.

Well, actually, there is only one proposal on the table for Tanaka Komuten to consider: to tie its near future with Atlas, in whatever form. One proposal does not constitute multiple choices, so this is an opportunity dichotomy trap. A decision means choosing the best alternative for reaching the goal with finite resources—and only one alternative means no decision is needed *yet*. Therefore, Tanaka Komuten is not at a decision point yet.

Some students would say that Tanaka Komuten needs to act immediately, because if it lets this opportunity go, there may not be another. Atlas might partner with someone else. Well, this is the fear of a passive person who waits for opportunity to bump into him or her. If we are proactive, always looking for continuous improvement, always looking for better ways to close the gaps between the current state and the goal, we will not indulge in such a fear and its accompanying false sense of urgency. We will be proactively looking for opportunities to continue our profitable growth. Yes, Tanaka does need to act, but the action should be to generate good alternatives for its own future.

So, the next thing the Tanakas should do is reconfirm their long-term goal and baseline, and make sure the goal and baseline are shared by all members in the company. Then, they should determine the most important gap between their current state and their future desired state, and generate multiple alternatives to close the gap, so that they can make a better decision. Maybe in the end, a joint venture with Atlas will turn out to be the best decision, but without any basis for comparison they will never know, and they will doubt themselves in the future. The process of generating alternatives is also a reality check—they will know what's possible and whether a joint venture with Atlas is really the best choice.

Other students argue that Tanaka Komuten should go with Atlas even though there is only one alternative, because the amount of investment is quite small and very manageable in the company's current financial condition. It is not a big risk. But even though the initial investment is small, the commitment could increase later and trigger a sunk cost trap followed by a further escalation of commitment. Because Tanaka Komuten is a family business, and senior management cares greatly about the family reputation, the Tanakas will not admit defeat. Instead, they will pour more resources into the projects that bear their name until they are completed successfully. Their small initial investment could thus potentially grow into a resource drain.

There is always the opportunity cost to consider, too. If Tanaka Komuten allows itself to be lured into a decision when it has only one alternative, it will have fallen into the second most common managerial decision trap: the opportunity trap. It will have started its decision-making process at a good opportunity, instead of at the goal to be achieved.

Of course, it takes resources to come up with alternative solutions and investigate them—just as students, when making a career decision, need to spend time and money to apply for jobs or higher education in order to generate job offers and university admission offers. Tanaka Komuten needs to use its finite resources to come up with alternatives concerning the most important gap that must be closed between its current state and the goal. What is its most important gap to close right now? The opportunity gap. Because of the decline of the construction industry in Japan, there are fewer opportunities, even though Tanaka Komuten's performance is still very strong. In order to achieve its goal of sustained success, the company's current priority should be to generate more opportunities—so its capabilities and performance can be utilized.

But we mustn't forget that the company's baseline—its image and reputation in Japan—must also be protected. To do this, the company may consider diversifying geographically or into other businesses in Japan that offer more opportunities to utilize its core competence and sustain the company's good image. If Tanaka explores geographic diversification, it needs to take into account that there are more than 100 countries in the world and the construction business is a relatively local business with many local requirements, such as building codes, climate, sources of building materials, and sources of labor. The best countries for it will therefore be those that will offer multiple opportunities in the future, so that the lessons learned from the first experience can be taken advantage of.

Once the top countries or areas are chosen, the next thing to do is to spend some resources to generate alternatives in those countries that would allow Tanaka Komuten's outstanding construction performance to bring sustained, profitable growth. This could include finding a competent local partner who can source opportunities, choosing another Japanese partner with complementary capabilities, going with Atlas, going in alone, and so on. Each alternative will carry different benefits, costs, risks, and incentives. The company also needs to be very clear that all alternatives to be considered should be above its baseline, and sustain the company's image and reputation.

This case study illustrates how easy it is to fall into the dichotomy opportunity trap and only ask, "Is this joint venture good or bad?" Tanaka Komuten must look instead at its long-term goal, as it seems that internally it has not yet agreed upon its goal and priorities. It probably has an unconscious goal of "sustainable, profitable growth", because that is what every business wants. Diversification is one of the ways to achieve this goal. It probably also has an unconscious baseline of "sustaining a good image for the company and family." Specialization has, in the past, been one of the ways of protecting this baseline. The company needs to state its goal and baseline explicitly and identify its current state so that it can determine which gap it needs to close. Tanaka Komuten is not lacking in performance for now; the real issue is the shrinking opportunities in Japan's construction market. But why is the company only looking at Brazil and Singapore projects with Atlas? Without alternatives, it really is not yet at the decision stage.

You can see the importance of proactively generating alternatives for ourselves when we have extra resources (time and money) to spend on it, so that we will not be put in a position in the future where we have no choices. Let's move on to the last GPA component: Alternatives.

CHAPTER 5

GPA: A for Alternatives

So far in the book, we've discussed some important points about decision making and alternatives. Before we go on to discuss alternatives further, let me recap those points briefly:

1. Decision making is not about go/no-go choices. It is about choosing the best of a wide range of different, "doable" alternatives.

2. The book *Smart Choices* said it well: "A decision cannot be better than the best alternative" (p. 7). So, if we want to make better decisions, we must first generate better alternatives.

3. All decisions are subject to change if better alternatives come along.

4. The best alternative is often a composite of different creative ideas.

THE IMPORTANCE OF ALTERNATIVES

After we have a clear long-term goal and have prioritized our short-term and mid-term objectives to achieve that goal, the next step is to consider the best alternatives for achieving our objectives. As we discussed in the previous chapter, we will never know if a decision is the best if we only consider one alternative. And as we mentioned just now, a decision cannot be better than the best alternative and all decisions are subject to change if better alternatives come along. If we've set clear goals and priorities, the more alternatives we have, the better our decision will be.

A decision cannot be better than the best alternative

It may be that pure luck has carried us along well so far, but we cannot count on luck to sustain us indefinitely in the future. Pure luck is not replicable. However, we *can* create what we might call "repeatable luck"—which is really preparation encountering good opportunities. We can maintain a state of preparedness through continuous improvements, and we can generate opportunities for ourselves that will enable us to be lucky.

So, there are two stages relating to alternatives in the GPA IPO framework:

1. Generating alternatives
2. Choosing the best of the alternatives generated

We need to consciously separate these two stages and involve different types of people in each. The first stage requires people who are credible "outsiders" and do not have much vested interest in the decision. They can help us think creatively and generate more innovative and diverse alternatives outside of our comfort zone. The second stage requires people who have had experience in similar situations, and can thus help us to consider the likely outcome and consequences of each alternative.

The best time to generate alternatives is when things are going well, because we are in a position to generate more and better alternatives, and can afford to spend resources generating alternatives that may not be immediately required.

While we cannot carry out every alternative that occurs to us, as our resources are finite, we should not put ourselves into a position where we have no choices. The process of coming up with alternatives also functions as a reality check. It resembles the job search process, in that it helps us recognize our strengths and weaknesses, learn more about specific areas that need improvement, and find out what possibilities exist in our current situation.

But what constitutes a "good" alternative?

QUALITY ALTERNATIVES

Good alternatives must be doable and capable of achieving our goal without creating unmanageable consequences. More importantly, however, good alternatives are:

1. Innovative
2. Significantly different from each other

All progress comes from change, even though not all changes bring progress—just as not all experiments succeed. No improvements can be made if there is no innovation: repeating the past will not lead to a better future. And it's vital that the alternatives we have to choose from differ significantly.

Here's an example. I have an MBA student who comes from a family of medical doctors. His parents always wanted him to become a doctor; however, he disliked the idea of making medicine his profession, because he prefers to see healthy people when he goes to work every day. So he asked his parents to give him the freedom to choose his own career. His parents were very puzzled by this request for freedom of choice, as they thought they had already provided it—after all, he could choose to be a cardiologist, a neurosurgeon, a gynecologist, an ophthalmologist, a pediatrician, a cytologist, a pathologist, a radiologist, and so on! But this MBA student's choices were not limited to specialities within the field of medicine—he could decide on something entirely different.

We are all "frogs in the bottom of a well"—the difference is where the well is located and how wide the opening is. To a frog in the "medicine" well, there are many choices, and the differences between cardiologist and gynecologist seem very significant. Yet there are even bigger differences between the fields of medicine, music, astronomy, history, and engineering, once one gets out of the well of medicine.

It is difficult to imagine other possibilities if we are never exposed to people and processes outside our own industry or country, as our imagination is often limited by our experience and exposure. We need to invite "foreign frogs" into our wells, so to speak, to stir up our imaginations by telling us what other people are doing. This will help us stay innovative and creative. It's also worth pointing out again that the best alternatives are often composites of creative ideas from several different people. My MBA student's best career choice might well have been some combination of medicine and business, for example.

FORCED AND VOLUNTARY INNOVATION

Innovation is often thought to come from inspiration. However, many studies have indicated that in fact innovation is one part inspiration and two parts discipline. Peter F. Drucker's well-known *Harvard Business Review* article "The Discipline of Innovation" lists seven sources for innovation:

1. Unexpected occurrences
2. Incongruities
3. Process needs
4. Industry and market changes
5. Demographic changes
6. Changes in perceptions
7. New knowledge

Basically, all these changes force people to get out of their comfort zone and innovate. Complacency is very natural and comfortable; few people love to innovate, and most only change when they are forced to.

Even the new information brought to light by research and development teams is spurred by the pressure to "publish or perish." If there is no pressure, we tend to maintain the status quo. Hence, the Chinese have a saying: "Wealth will not pass beyond the third generation" (富不过三代)—not because the members of the third generation are any less intelligent than the previous two, but because there is less pressure on them, and they have less sense of urgency and discipline. The grandparents usually spoil the grandkids instead of disciplining them. Their complacency or lack of a sense of urgency will mean they are be surpassed by other people who *are* pressured to change, who *have to* innovate in order to survive. It is really sad: if we do not have the self-discipline to innovate and continuously improve, we will surely be left behind by others who do. The best way to counter complacency is to put pressure on yourself to innovate in good times and bad until innovation becomes a habit, and even a hobby.

Leaders have a responsibility to establish a corporate culture that encourages and demands that every employee innovate at all times, to constantly observe, think, and experiment. Encourage innovative experiments; allow failures, but demand progress. As Sir Arthur C. Clarke, British inventor and futurist, said, "The only way to discover the limits of the possible is to go beyond them into the impossible." Only when we make innovation the norm, the customary belief, the unstated assumption, the habit, and the hobby of a company, does it become part of the corporate culture—and that is the best antidote to extinction.

> *Encourage innovative experiments; allow failures, but demand progress*

ENCOURAGING INNOVATION

Innovation is about compelling ourselves to discover the impossibilities. In their book *When Sparks Fly*, Dorothy A. Leonard and Walter C. Swap state, "Creativity is a process of developing and expressing novel ideas that are likely to be useful."

In business, many innovative ideas and products are generated in rounds of brainstorming by diversified teams—creative groups that are heterogeneous with respect to abilities, skills, knowledge, culture, thinking styles, and perspectives. This is the reason that multinational companies like to have employees from various backgrounds. As we saw in the story of the MBA student earlier, our values and ideas are usually affected by which "well" we come from and the different experiences we have had, so inviting visits from "foreign frogs" can promote divergent thinking. External minds can challenge our judgments and beliefs by asking "Why not?" This clash of ideas encourages creative abrasion—not to be confused with interpersonal abrasion caused by the clash of people.

Among the techniques for stimulating creative ideas, *backcasting*, developed by Amory Lovins, chairman and chief scientist of the Rocky Mountain Institute, and *forced association*, developed by Alex Faickney Osborn, advertising manager and founder of the Creative Education Foundation, are the two I like most.

Backcasting is about projecting forward into the future, then looking back. Assume your decisions have had a very good or very bad result. What did you do and what happened? Let's use our example from Chapter 3 about the student who wanted to have the number-one company for children's clothing. Imagine it is five years from now, and his company actually has become the leading brand in children's clothing in his country. What decision did he make five years ago that allowed him to achieve his goal? Now imagine that, instead, his company has gone bankrupt—again, what decision did he make five years ago that led to this failure?

Forced association is about learning from others things that may seem irrelevant to our situations at the first glance, in order to force us to imagine and innovate—things like strategies and solutions used in other industries, other countries, and other companies. We need to see if their experiences could offer solutions for our situation. For instance, could my student learn from a soft-drink company, a mining company, or auto company in his or another country, and use its strategies to benefit his children's clothing business?

During a period of idea creation, judgment should be suspended or many creative ideas will be killed. Wild cards should be encouraged, and participants should be urged to build on others' ideas. We will use objective reasoning to choose the best ideas later; during idea creation, the aim is to come up with lots of innovative, significantly different ideas to choose from, to modify, to enhance, and to combine into the best possible alternative. So avoid criticism, as the process is as valuable as the outcome. Emphasize quantity first, quality later.

It is also good to keep a record of all the ideas generated, regardless of how foolish some may seem. Sometimes, the best idea looks foolish in the beginning.

During idea creation, it can be helpful if the manager is deliberately absent, as this prevents his or her opinion interfering with the flow of the participants' creative juices. A brainstorming session is a time to have fun and be temporarily irresponsible, as such an atmosphere allows people to get out of their box and think well. Stay alert for ideas at any moment.

Beware of idea-killers. Are any of these familiar to you?

- "That's against company policy."
- "Senior management will never sign off on that."
- "That's not within our area of responsibility."
- "Somebody has tried that before."
- "We're not quite ready for that."
- "It's great, but ahead of its time."
- "But what would you do about . . . ?"
- "That creates as many problems as it solves."
- "We'll never have time to do that."
- "You must be joking."
- "We have to be more realistic."
- "That would step on too many toes."
- "It will never fly."
- "Great idea—but not for us."
- "Here we go again."

And the universal idea-killer is silence: don't participate, don't think or contribute, don't challenge common wisdom. Remain silent.

Of course, time is a finite resource, so we cannot keep on producing ideas and alternatives without making decisions. We need to bear in mind that alternatives are generated for the purpose of closing the gap between our goal and our current situation. After we have enough creative alternatives, we should move on to the stage of objective reasoning, when we evaluate our alternatives and discuss their feasibility and consequences in order to choose the best one.

Usually, the best alternative is a composite of different creative ideas that:

- meet the business objectives
- respond to the real issues and challenges
- do not create unmanageable negative effects
- are doable.

COMMON FAILURES REGARDING ALTERNATIVES

One of the most common failures with respect to alternatives is that there is only one alternative or all the choices are just different variations of the same alternative. Discussing the viability of that single alternative is wasting time—time that should be used to generate more alternatives and ideas. Since the best alternative is usually a composite of different ideas, a quality decision can only be made when we have many alternatives from which to choose.

Sometimes, we miss great alternatives due to negative assumptions—wasting time discussing why particular alternatives are not doable instead of discussing how to make them doable.

In the idea creation stage, two common problems crop up. First, some or all of the team members may be lazy and not thinking or innovating. They let someone else come up with ideas and just say, "It all sounds good to me." Second, some may be insisting on their own ideas and indulging in pride of ownership, unwilling to let others modify and enhance them. To combat these problems, it is helpful to set up two rules before a brainstorming session:

1. No free rides. Here, we act in the spirit of George Bernard Shaw, famous Irish playwright, who said, "Few people think more than two or three times a year. I have made an international reputation for myself by thinking once or twice a week." Everyone at the session must have done some independent thinking first, come with several ideas and stated them at the beginning of the meeting. No comments or criticisms can be made at this time. Then, we will build on one another's ideas and think creatively.

2. No ownership of ideas. Once an idea is stated, it is public property. As there is no ownership, anyone can modify it, build upon it, discard it, enhance it, or combine it with other ideas.

Here are some helpful questions that we can use to find out if we have enough alternatives for the time being:

1. Do you have a range of significantly different alternatives (at least three)?
2. Are you satisfied with one of your existing alternatives or the combination of some existing alternatives as a final decision?
3. Do other elements of this decision-making process (e.g. objective reasoning) require your time and attention more?
4. Would time be more productively spent on other activities or decisions?

We can move on to the objective reasoning stage when we can answer "yes" to all these questions.

CASE STUDY

The situation: Leclerc Machines de Cuisine

Leclerc Machines de Cuisine, a Paris manufacturer of food processors, blenders, grinders, and other chef's supplies, has recently begun exporting its products to the United States through a sole US distributor, Creative Cuisines, Inc. (an Atlanta, Georgia, firm). Although Leclerc was at first reluctant to accept an exclusive distribution agreement, the company had finally been persuaded to do so when Creative Cuisines agreed to assume all marketing and sales promotion costs for the Leclerc line and to market the products aggressively.

It is quite a surprise, then, when Creative Cuisines learns that someone else in the US—a mail-order firm calling itself Reliable Restaurant and Home Kitchen Supplies—has begun to place ads in consumer magazines and trade journals. They are offering the Leclerc LMC Professional and LMC Standard food processors at prices considerably lower than those of Creative Cuisines.

The president of Creative Cuisines, Mr. Bill Lewis, immediately calls Leclerc when he learns of the ads, to see if somehow Leclerc is responsible. Leclerc's overseas sales manager, Mr. Francois Jost, says that Leclerc has not authorized a sale to Reliable and expresses his dismay that Reliable has managed to receive shipments.

Mr. Lewis then proceeds to investigate Reliable, but with little success. He learns only that they are a New Jersey company specializing in mail-order discount kitchen supplies. His next step is to consult his firm's attorney, Ms. Marie Dominic, to determine what legal action could be taken.

Dialogue: A parallel import problem

Characters: Mr. Bill Lewis, President, Creative Cuisines, Inc.

Ms. Marie Dominic, attorney representing Creative Cuisines

Mr. Lewis and Ms. Dominic are meeting in Ms. Dominic's office to discuss possible legal action against Reliable Restaurant and Home Kitchen Supplies.

Dominic:	From what you told me on the phone, Bill, this sounds like a clear-cut case of parallel import.
Lewis:	Is that legal?
Dominic:	It depends on how Reliable is getting the Leclerc products.
Lewis:	What do you mean?
Dominic:	If Reliable is getting its products direct from Leclerc in violation of your exclusive distribution agreement, it's illegal. And it's illegal if the Leclerc products it's selling are counterfeits, not genuine Leclerc products.
Lewis:	Well, Leclerc claims to have no knowledge of the shipments.
Dominic:	Are the products genuine?
Lewis:	They seem to be. We're getting one this week, and believe me, we'll take the thing apart if we have to in order to determine whether it's genuine.
Dominic:	Okay, that's a good step. If they aren't genuine, you both—Leclerc and you—have a case.
Lewis:	My feeling, though, is that they really are Leclerc products. They're offering a manufacturer's warranty. Hey, that's illegal isn't it?
Dominic:	Not necessarily.
Lewis:	What?
Dominic:	Well, if Reliable is offering a manufacturer's warranty, then Leclerc has to honor it. As long as the goods are legitimate.
Lewis:	But we're the only authorized service center in the US
Dominic:	True, but Reliable could send the food processors directly to Leclerc or to the distributor from whom they purchased the products.
Lewis:	I don't know about that. On the warranty the return card is printed with our address. We maintain all of that information here.
Dominic:	They might have had their own warranty cards printed; there is also a possibility that they could just have all the service done by you. Do you know all of the customers who bought your supplies?
Lewis:	No. But we can institute a careful check. I'm sure that there must be some way to find out who bought Creative Cuisine–supplied processors.

Dominic: What are we talking about in terms of loss in sales revenue?

Lewis: Well, I don't know what Reliable's sales are. But our sales are off about 30 percent this month.

Dominic: Is that unusual for July?

Lewis: Not in general. But I don't know with this product. We only started distributing it in January. Our forecast calls for a steady increase in sales. But that's beside the point. What can we legally do to stop these pirates?

Dominic: First, I'll write a letter to Reliable implying possible illegalities. Meanwhile, you see what you can find out about Reliable's source of supply. Get Leclerc to issue a warning to its foreign distributors. Most likely one of its own distributors, maybe in Canada or in Europe, is supplying Reliable with products. That happens quite often. In many cases the distributor doesn't even know he's violating an agreement. The truth is, though, these measures may be ineffective. I suggest you immediately adopt some marketing tactics to counter this offensive, the same way you would with any other competitive threat.

Discussion

Before Creative Cuisines jumps into a legal battle or a price war with Reliable, it should pause and think through its decision-making process again, starting with its goal (which should always be the starting point, no exceptions). The logical business goal of Creative Cuisines—and, indeed, of any business—is sustained, profitable growth. As we mentioned in Chapter 3, it's not necessary to have a fancy, creative business goal, only to be creative in thinking up ways to achieve that goal.

Then, Creative Cuisines needs to consider what its current priority is. What is the most important gap to close between the company's current state and its goal of sustained, profitable growth? Is the company 1) lacking in opportunities to compete, or 2) lacking performance good enough to beat the competition? In this situation, we can see that Creative does not lack opportunities to compete, because it is supposed to have 100 percent of the opportunity to sell Leclerc's products. Therefore, it must be lacking in performance. What specific gap in performance does Creative have that caused it to lose its 100 percent opportunity to compete?

Opportunities arise from unmet needs. In this situation, the main party with unmet needs is the customers.

A customer's need is always to buy the desired product at a lower price, and Reliable met this need better than Creative Cuisines. So the business naturally went to Reliable. Customers don't really care who the legal distributor is, as long as they can get the products they want at a lower price, with the same warranty.

The reason Reliable could sell the same product at a lower price is that it used a low-cost distribution channel—mail and phone order—rather than bearing the cost of retail shops and the marketing cost for promoting the Leclerc brand. And, from the customer's perspective, this alternative distribution channel is more convenient than visiting retail shops.

Of course, the obvious solution is to shut down Reliable by legal means, but since Reliable is selling genuine Leclerc products and did not get the products directly from Leclerc, a legal battle will not close the performance gap for Creative Cuisines. On the contrary, Creative will spend lots of resources (both time and money) to benefit an irrelevant third party, the attorney's office, without improving its own performance. Wouldn't Creative's finite resources be better used to benefit itself, instead? Creative's priority at this stage is to close its performance gap and gain back its opportunities.

Creative needs to generate multiple alternatives for closing its performance gap. For example:

- Creating its own mail-order and phone-order channel to compete with Reliable
- Working with Reliable—Reliable could become one of Creative's distribution channels
- Working with another mail-order firm to compete with Reliable
- Finding ways to differentiate the offers through the retail channel and mail/phone-order channel to maintain the value of each
- Creating more channels (e.g. the internet, or alliances with other retail chains or associations)

Unless Creative can meet customers' unmet needs proactively with outstanding performance, it will continue to allow competitors to thrive in the marketplace. Spending its finite resources to defeat a competitor without enhancing its own performance or opportunities is not the way to achieve sustained, profitable growth!

Consider this, as well: Reliable is not the only mail-order company in America. Why didn't anyone at Creative think about using multiple channels? Perhaps someone did, and the sole-distributor agreement made Creative too complacent to consider it as an option. Or perhaps the mail-order idea was shut down internally because management knew it could cause channel conflicts internally and was too lazy to think of ways to prevent this. If Creative does not proactively innovate and change, it will certainly be surpassed by competitors, whether through proper or improper means.

If parallel importation of Leclerc products continues or increases in spite of any response Creative makes to satisfy market needs, it will probably be due to the unmet needs of another party: the Leclerc company. A manufacturer always needs to sell more of its products.

Leclerc may not have a strict contract with all its distributors globally to prevent parallel imports, but where there's a will, there's a way. If Leclerc is willing to stop the parallel importation, it can. It simply needs to allocate resources to identify the source of the imported products and institute appropriate penalties to prevent and deter parallel importation. The problem should be solved from upstream, by the manufacturer, not from downstream, by the distributor. If the manufacturer is not willing to stop parallel imports, they will continue to occur. If this turns out to be the case, Creative should start generating other alternatives for its future.

Once we have multiple alternatives to close the gap between the current state and our goal, we are ready to choose the best alternative to achieve our goal with our finite resources. The next chapter will discuss how to use objective reasoning to do this. First, however, let's do a quick recap of the GPA part of the decision-making process, to help you incorporate it into your daily work.

SUMMARY OF GPA

We should build the habit of using GPA to approach all decisions. To practice GPA, we should ask ourselves three questions before starting work every day:

1. Does my work contribute to the team's shared goal?

   If the answer is no, please stop and ask yourself why. Maybe you don't clearly understand the team's shared goal. Maybe you just do what others ask, without knowing how your work fits in with the team's goal. Maybe you just do what has always been done without knowing why. You must stop and seek clarification courteously and diplomatically from your superior about why you are doing what you do and how your work contributes to the team goal. Otherwise, your work could be a waste of resources and you will not receive any appreciation upon its completion. Everything we do must contribute positively to the accomplishment of the team goal.

2. Is there something I should do that's more important than what I am about to do in order to reach our team goal?

   If the answer is yes, why don't you attend to the more important matter? Maybe you tend to follow other people's instructions without exercising your own judgment; maybe you have been proceeding according to habit, without any thought of priority. Either way, it is time to stop, think and ask questions (again, courteously and diplomatically) until you know that you are working on the most important thing first.

3. If you are already working on the most important matter for accomplishing the team's goal, then ask yourself the third question: is there a better way to do it?

   As time progresses and technology improves, there is usually a better way to accomplish the same thing. Spend some time using the observe-think-experiment process to try out new and better ways. There is always room for innovation, even for the most routine and mundane task.

One final point: perfection can be our goal, but is usually not a current alternative. We should not give up pursuing perfection just because the current reality is not perfect; nor should we abandon the current reality to pursue a perfection which does not yet exist.

To put it another way: we must not create a false choice between G (goal) and A (alternatives) in the framework. Instead, we must choose the best alternative to achieve the goal. For example, some people give up pursuing their dream job because their current job is less than perfect; others quit an imperfect job to pursue a dream job that is not yet available to them. We should do neither. Rather, we should choose the best job available now in order to pursue that perfect job in the future. Alternatives are implementable options, not wishful thinking. Choose the best alternative among those available to pursue your goal, even if sometimes the best alternative is not good enough. As Theodore Roosevelt, the 26th President of the United States, once said, "Do what you can, with what you have, where you are."

CHAPTER 6

IPO: O for Objective Reasoning

A quality decision requires process quality, and the three keys to process quality are information (I), people (P), and objective reasoning (O). In other words, we need to know the following:

1. What information should we gather in order to make timely adjustments to our decision, since all decisions are subject to change in the face of better alternatives?
2. Who should be involved in the decision-making process?
3. How can we evaluate multiple alternatives and choose the best one to achieve our goal?

At this point, I want to again make it clear that this decision-making framework is not a strict procedure or process, and thus has no particular sequence, except that the starting point should always be the goal. So, although I use the acronym IPO, you can see I will be describing the components in a different order, beginning with objective reasoning (O).

You may ask, "So why use IPO at all then?" Well, as I mentioned before, I use the IPO acronym to remind us that all decisions are subject to change, just as a company's share price changes immediately after its initial public offering (IPO) even though the initial price was a deliberate and conscious decision. The price will continue to change due to internal and external conditions.

Let me explain. I practiced my decision-making framework in Asia, where "face" is very important to managers, and I discovered that many managers were using finite resources to maintain decisions which had become outdated. They felt that changing or questioning their previous decisions would cause them to "lose face". However, using the analogy of a stock IPO, I was able to remove the idea of "face" from the equation. We make the best decision we can today, given today's situation; tomorrow is a new situation and a new day. Tomorrow, today's decision may become obsolete because of some major change in the marketplace. Just as a stock often trades at a different price even on its first day on the market, so also our business decisions may need to be readjusted immediately after we make them. This is not a matter of "face"; rather, it is a matter of business reality. It's wise to change when the conditions relating to our previous decision have changed; it is foolish not to change if the time and conditions have changed.

We have already seen how to use GPA to set a shared goal, to prioritize the allocation of resources and to generate many, different options for achieving the goal. The next logical step in the decision-making process is to use objective reasoning to choose from among those alternatives. So, let's look first at the topic of objective reasoning. Then, we will discuss the matters of information and people.

Objective reasoning is essential for decision making. It is how we choose the best alternative to reach our final decision, so it is the most important link to the future implementation of our decision. If we can do a thorough job of it, we will have made the best preparation for the implementation of our decision: there should be very few surprises during implementation, and we will significantly increase the odds of success. So, while objective reasoning may take some time to do, it saves a lot of time later.

WHAT IS OBJECTIVE REASONING?

Objective reasoning is evaluating the potential outcomes of each alternative when implemented, so that we can choose the best alternative.

To put it another way, objective reasoning is the process that converts each alternative into potential positive and negative consequences. Good decision making means choosing the alternative that will bring the most desirable consequences. In a sense, decision making is not about choosing a certain action; rather, it is about choosing the consequences of

Decision making is not about choosing a certain action; rather, it is about choosing the consequences of that action

that action. And since decision making is resource allocation, it is our resource allocation that must generate positive consequences. If there will be no positive consequences from a resource allocation, it is an inconsequential decision and a waste of resources.

We must also remember that all decisions are about the future, and the future is unknown and uncertain. Thus, each decision is an experiment and carries risks that we must assess. We need to be conscientious about the impact a decision will have and allocate resources to manage the risks. If we don't, we may make irresponsible decisions.

HOW DO WE DO OBJECTIVE REASONING?

Since objective reasoning is about choosing the alternative that will have the best consequences, we first need to prioritize our alternatives according to their positive and negative consequences. We can do this using the following matrix.

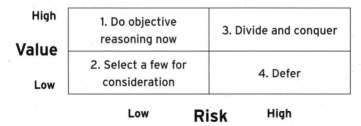

In the top left quadrant, the alternatives that have a high value and low risk are our first priority, and objective reasoning should be done for them right away.

The bottom left is for low-value and low-risk alternatives. We can consider combining a few of these options, based on our available resources, if this will cause their aggregated value to increase without increasing the risks. However, we should not allocate finite resources to them at the expense of our first-priority alternatives.

In the top right quadrant go the high-value and high-risk alternatives. These need more innovation to achieve and are often best approached by taking small, experimental steps—also known as "dividing and conquering." For example, one alternative for the Creative Cuisines company in the last chapter would be to launch its own brand of cooking equipment instead of remaining the distributor for Leclerc. This alternative has high value but also high risk, so Creative should divide it into smaller steps. Perhaps it could start by creating a small, innovative attachment for Leclerc's equipment under the Creative brand, in order to work out its manufacturing capability and processes and get the brand into the marketplace. Then it could continuously adjust, improve and add components, with the aim of eventually offering an entire product line of its own.

In the bottom right are the alternatives with the lowest priority—those with high risk and low value. These should be deferred from consideration.

After we've prioritized our alternatives, we start doing objective reasoning for the alternatives with the highest priority (those with high value and low risk):

1. We assess the alternative's positive consequences in light of our goals:
   - What are the potential positive consequences this alternative will generate?
   - If we can successfully execute this alternative, are the outcomes really what we want?
   - How important are they in helping us to achieve our goal?
2. We assess the cost of bringing these positive consequences into being:

- Do we have the necessary resources to implement this alternative?
- What is the probability that we will succeed?
- Could we increase the probability of success with more resources?
- Are we willing and able to increase our resource allocation?

3. We evaluate the alternative's negative consequences:
   - What are the potential negative consequences this alternative could generate?
   - What is the probability that these negative consequences will happen?
   - What impact will these negative consequences have on achieving our goal?

4. We assess the remedies for these negative consequences:
   - Are there ways to prevent, eliminate, mitigate, or manage these negative consequences?
   - Do we have the resources to implement these remedies?
   - Are we willing and able to allocate resources to implement these remedies?

Dr. Joyce Brothers, an American psychologist and advice columnist, once gave a simple rule of thumb I find helpful: "If you can take the worst; take the risk."

We need to look at the resource requirements for the implementation of our priority-one alternatives, to the point where we have at least an idea of what the necessary resources are, where they would come from, and where we would allocate them. Almost all dreams can come true with sufficient resources, and nightmares can be managed given enough resources. During objective reasoning, new ideas may also be generated about how to maximize positive consequences and minimize negative consequences.

Responsible decision makers must also choose a course of action with open eyes, aware of the potential impacts and consequences and how available resources can be used most wisely. In other words, they must use objective reasoning to fully prepare for the successful implementation and minimize the possible negative consequences of their decision. As

Preparation for execution starts during this stage of the decision-making process, not after the decision is made

John R. Wooden, famous American basketball coach, said, "Failure to prepare is preparing to fail." Preparation for execution starts during this stage of the decision-making process, not after the decision is made.

If we don't do objective reasoning *before* we make our final decision, we may make an irresponsible decision—for ourselves and for others. We could wind up with no dreams, only nightmares. We may push the responsibility away, but we cannot push the consequences away.

During the objective reasoning phase, we need to involve different people than those who helped generate the ideas. We need people with expertise and experience—people who have "been there, done that," and can objectively evaluate the consequences.

COMMON FAILURES IN OBJECTIVE REASONING

One of the most common failures in objective reasoning is simply that people do not do it. They think that once a decision is made, their dream will just come true somehow. But it takes very conscious allocation of adequate resources to fulfill a dream. Good intentions, sheer determination, and luck are not enough: it will take conscious effort and continuous improvement to produce optimal outcome.

Some people are unwilling to bear the responsibility of decision making. However, making no decision is actually making a decision to maintain the status quo, which also has consequences. We may be able to escape the responsibility, but we cannot escape the consequences. For instance, say that I don't want to bear the responsibility of driving, so I decide to hire a driver. Even though it is the responsibility of the driver to ensure the safety of his or her passengers, if the driver is reckless and there's an accident, the passengers will suffer the consequences also. So, even though I'm not responsible for driving, I am still responsible for choosing a careful driver.

Some may say that an accident might still happen even if I hire a responsible driver. Well, yes: some accidents are totally unpredictable and out of our control, such as a tree suddenly falling on the car. But a decision maker is only responsible for managing risks, not unknowns. For the unknown, no one can be held accountable. Another example: earthquakes are a known risk, but when an earthquake will hit is unknown. If a city is located in a known earthquake zone, the city government must be responsible for allocating resources to prepare the city for earthquakes, in order to minimize damage if and when an earthquake hits. It might institute special building codes, create emergency plans, conduct special safety education, provide training on what to do during an earthquake, and so on. But the city government is not responsible for predicting when an earthquake will hit, because this is an unknown. They simply need to be ready whenever it hits.

One final word: don't be deterred just because the future is uncertain. There are always risks; we simply need to know what the risks are and manage them. There are many books worth reading that provide useful approaches to risk management—by, for example, diluting the risk, diversifying the risk, hedging the risk, sharing the risk, or insuring against the risk. Ensure that you are aware of the most relevant approaches in your industry, and apply them.

CASE STUDY

The situation: Comtec Corporation

Comtec Corporation, a small manufacturer of industrial microcomputers and application-specific software in Cambridge, Massachusetts, is having a difficult time competing in both the domestic and international markets. Sales of its primary product, the Comtec 100 Microcomputer, are slow, and the company's profit is practically nonexistent. In short, Comtec is facing a serious financial crisis.

In an attempt to save the company, the president, Dr. Daniel Needham, has hired an outside consultant, Ms. Roberta Malcolm, a seasoned professional with years of high-tech marketing experience. After studying the situation for a couple of weeks, Ms. Malcolm has made three recommendations. The first is to close down the European sales office in Amsterdam and concentrate, for the present at least, on the US market. The second recommendation is for Comtec to shift from a hardware to a software emphasis; specifically, Ms. Malcolm has advised the company to begin producing Windows-compatible software for general-purpose laboratory and technical uses. Her third recommendation calls for the company to shift its advertising and sales promotion from a heavy reliance on journal advertising and press releases to direct-mail advertising and trade show exhibits.

All three conclusions, though not explicitly critical of the vice president for sales and marketing, Mr. Harry Otto, are implicitly so, since Mr. Otto was instrumental in implementing the present marketing strategy. It is now up to the company to decide whether or not to accept any or all of the consultant's recommendations.

Dialogue: A new marketing strategy?

Characters: Dr. Daniel Needham, President, Comtec Corporation
Mr. Harry Otto, Vice President, Comtec Corporation
Ms. Roberta Malcolm, Computer Consultant

The three are discussing Ms. Malcolm's report in Dr. Needham's office at Comtec.

Malcolm: Let me just say at the beginning that I realize my recommendations may seem very bold, but given the present financial situation at Comtec, I think bold measures are needed.

Otto: Right on both counts. The question is, are these the right measures? My feeling is simply that we haven't been aggressive enough in our marketing. Also, the new targeted fields—materials-testing automation and chromatography automation—are not quick sells; it takes some time to build up orders. We launched our new campaign in the early fall and it's just January now. I think you're premature in your assessment that this is not the right market.

Needham: Harry's right to some extent, but the truth is the orders just aren't coming in fast enough. We can't play a long-term waiting game. We don't have the capital to last.

Otto: All right. Orders aren't coming in in the necessary quantity, but we're getting more and more inquiries, and with proper action we should be able to turn them into orders.

Malcolm: Mr. Otto, I understand your position, but I don't feel that you've received enough inquiries to warrant optimism.

Otto: I'm not that optimistic at all about it, but I feel we have to give this market, this product, some chance.

Needham: Harry, what are you basing your sales projections on?

Otto: First, our sales manager in Amsterdam, Max Mendel, is right now working on an order for 10 Comtecs, plus software. That amounts to $200,000.

Malcolm: But an order isn't an order until you get a Purchase Order number.

Otto: Right. But Max feels confident he'll get it.

Needham: That brings up the whole matter of the European sales office.

Malcolm: Yes, it does. I can't see that it's worth keeping. It doesn't even pay for itself.

Needham: Well, I don't think that's true. But it barely pays for itself.

Otto: Ms. Malcolm's correct, Dan. It hasn't paid for itself in four months. I still don't feel that means we should shut it down. The potential is there. Max is a good sales rep, and things are beginning to turn.

Malcolm: Gentlemen, let me make a couple of things clear. I was hired by you to do a study and make some recommendations. I did that. It's your choice whether to accept the recommendations or not. I happen to think my recommendations are sound, but it's up to you to decide. The reasons I think they are sound are detailed in the report, but let me just reiterate a few facts here. First, in three months of active effort you have only six orders. Second, the competition, particularly in chromatography, is keen. Third, the European sales office is costing more than it's producing. Fourth, your microcomputer is too expensive, given the fact that an IBM PC costs one-fourth as much as the Comtec and is an industry standard. Granted, it may not do as much, but it is basically all most researchers need, given the right software. If you convert your software so that it will run on a Windows operating system, you'll be in a position to do just that. And if you are more horizontal than vertical in your approach to the market, you'll have a larger target. Fifth, your advertising and sales promotion measures are not getting to the right people. Buy some lists and then do a direct-mail shot. Go to every trade show you can and demonstrate your product. The audience you're trying to reach doesn't take journal advertising seriously. They want more information than they can get in an ad. Direct mail can give that to them; mailing out a demo can generate even more purchase orders.

Needham: How much would a direct mail campaign like that cost? What sort of resources would be needed to make a quality demo? Can we afford that right now?

Malcolm: It can't be more expensive than bleeding from the European office for another six months. The demo market is pretty competitive. If you order a large batch, you can get them priced pretty low.

Otto: Well, I think that making a sharp demo and maybe sending teams out with it to trade shows could be a good idea. But we will need to do some research into the pricing. Did you give us a list of reputable suppliers for making the demos? Did you include a list of the best trade shows for us to attend? Or do we need to put someone from our company on that? Do you have any other suggestions? Is there anything else we can do to turn things around? It seems that these suggestions don't really give us many choices.

Discussion

First, let me note that three recommendations do not constitute enough alternatives for a situation as dire as the one at Comtec; there should be more. However, we can use these three to illustrate objective reasoning. First, let's prioritize them. The first was closing down the European sales office in Amsterdam and concentrating, for the present, on the US market. This seems to be a high-value, low-risk alternative, so we should consider it now.

The second recommendation was for Comtec to shift from a hardware to a software emphasis. Specifically, the suggestion was for Comtec to give up its special hardware and convert its software to run on general-purpose PC hardware with Windows-based software. This alternative seems to be a high-value and high-risk alternative, so we would need to divide it into smaller pieces to test its feasibility and odds of success. We can do objective reasoning on this thereafter.

Ms. Malcolm's third recommendation was that the company shift its advertising and sales promotion from a heavy reliance on journal advertising and press releases to direct-mail advertising and trade show exhibits. This alternative seems to be relatively low-value and low-risk, so we can consider it if we have sufficient resources. We should do objective reasoning on it later.

We will do objective reasoning on the first-priority recommendation: to close down the European sales office in Amsterdam and concentrate on the US market. Let's work through the four steps mentioned earlier:

1. **What are the positive consequences?** That the company will stop losing money on the European office, which cannot pay for itself, and concentrate on the US market.
2. **What's the cost of bringing these positive consequences into being?** To answer this question, we need to answer a number of other questions: What action is needed to "stop the bleeding"? Should Comtec lay off European staff and negotiate the early termination of the office lease? Does the company have the resources needed for severance pay? Does it have the resources to pay the early termination penalty in the office lease? Where will these resources come from? And if it has the needed resources, will this help the company to achieve its goal?

   In terms of concentrating on the US market: What resources does it take to do this? Does Comtec have these resources? Where will the resources be coming from? Where will they be going? If the company transferred the European staff to the US, will there be enough savings? Closing down the European office may "stop the bleeding", but it will not generate new blood for the US. So, what is the value of this action to achieving our goal?
3. **What are the negative consequences?** They could include losing all potential orders in Europe, giving the company a negative image

both in Europe and in the US, and making any later re-entry into Europe more difficult.

4. **Do we have remedies for these consequences?** What resources does it take to implement these remedies? Where would the resources come from and go to?

It's obvious now that this seemingly high-value, low-risk alternative is not so high value and not so low risk, and that Comtec's management needs to generate more ideas on how to "stop the bleeding" without negatively impacting the company's potential orders and image. The European office cannot be closed abruptly without hurting the US market, so Comtec needs to find other ways to restructure. The savings from the restructure can then be used to experiment with Ms. Malcolm's second recommendation.

You can see that while objective reasoning takes time, it's time very well spent to prevent making irresponsible decisions, decisions that cannot be successfully implemented, and decisions that will not get us closer to the goal even if successfully executed. Now, let's go on to examine how to find the information we need to make timely adjustments to our decisions, in order to bring about the best overall outcome.

CHAPTER 7

IPO: I for Information

To make good decisions with objective reasoning—and later to make any necessary adjustments to those decisions—we need to collect relevant, correct, explicit, and "total picture" information. Information is another key component in quality decision making.

LOOKING BACK TO LOOK FORWARD

Progress is not made by repeating the past, but unfortunately, history does tend to repeat itself if we don't learn from it. All the decisions we make are subject to change and adjustment. First, we have to recognize the difference between today's reality and the assumptions we made previously about today. Then we must be proactive about making modifications to our decisions, instead of waiting for circumstances or someone else to force us to change. And since no one can roll back time to collect the information in the past that we need now, we need to be forward-thinking, and start to collect the data now that we will need to make future decisions.

Collecting information takes resources, sometimes a lot of resources; therefore, we need to allocate those resources responsibly. Whenever we are making a decision, we need to think about what information we will need to make the next decision. We need to ask ourselves, "How might I change my decision for the better in the future? What information will I need to adjust my decision? How will I collect it? How will I use it once it is collected?"

Today's world is flooded with all kinds of information. Some is only noise; some is useful. We cannot make good decisions based on useless information, however, so we must be able to differentiate between useful and useless information.

> *The most misleading information is factual but partial information*

Sometimes, the information is useful but does not give us the whole picture. The most misleading information is factual but partial information: information needs to be complete to give us a proper view of the issue. This is the foundation for making the right decision.

Here's an example. When I went to study in the US in the early 1970s, I encountered a certain diet soda for the first time. This diet drink claimed to help people lose weight. Well, I wanted to find out the relationship between drinking that diet soda and weight, so I spent a week taking notes at the university cafeteria. My data showed that more than 80 percent of students buying the diet soda at the cafeteria were overweight. Then I conducted another study among my classmates who were overweight. Nearly 99 percent of them drank that diet drink. I arrived at the following conclusion: the drink made people fat, because almost all the fat people were drinking it, and the majority of those who drank it were fat.

The conclusion is questionable without doubt, yet my data was accurate. How could accurate information lead to misleading conclusions? Because my information was partial. I had no data for comparison on whether those people would be more overweight if they drank regular soda. I should have conducted a control experiment: if the overweight people drank the original drink formula instead of the diet version, did they become heavier? When we are collecting information, we need the total picture—the entire movie, not just a few sound bites.

Many news reports and market research reports offer real but partial information. They can be used for reference, but not for decision making. In the case of market surveys, we need to understand who answered the survey, under what circumstances the survey was answered, and exactly how the survey questions were phrased before we include the data in our decision-making process. Many market surveys merely provide "confirming evidence" for a preconceived idea or a foregone conclusion. Even if the survey was done with a high degree of scientific discipline, we cannot base our decision solely on the survey result, because there is one big unknown: whether people's actual actions are consistent with their answers to the survey.

INFORMATION COLLECTION THAT WASTES CORPORATE RESOURCES

Many professionals consider collecting information in order to answer frequent, ad hoc questions from management to be the biggest problem in their daily work life. This kind of information collection wastes large amounts of corporate resources, especially time resources. In the classroom, professors often tell students that there are no stupid questions— and in a learning environment, any question *is* a good question, because questions help students to learn, which is their primary goal. However, in business situations, there are definitely stupid questions. "Stupid" management questions are inconsequential questions, in that answering them will not lead to progress or the achievement of organizational goals. Perhaps management does not have any intention of doing anything with the answer, and the question was asked merely to satisfy personal curiosity. Well, there are better ways to satisfy personal curiosity than wasting corporate resources.

Every question from a manager will send subordinates on a quest for the answer. Managers should have enough self-awareness to realize that their questions cannot be treated casually by subordinates, and so organizational resources will be spent to answer them. If a question is framed incorrectly, or leads nowhere, or if the answer will not matter because no one will do anything with the answer, then precious finite resources will be wasted and subordinates will inevitably feel frustrated and disoriented. Productivity and morale will be negatively impacted.

Before casually asking a question which will send your team on a quest to collect a lot of information, ask yourself, "How will I use the answer? Is the answer to this question necessary to make management decisions which will lead to progress and the achievement of team goals?" If the answer is no, don't ask it now. And if the answer could be useful later, maybe you should ask the question later—outdated information could be very misleading.

Questions from leaders also imply certain focuses to subordinates, and will orient them in a certain direction. Leaders and managers should thus stop themselves from making irresponsible inquiries that will disorient their team.

Responsible questions, by contrast, will orient the team members in the right direction and focus them on the important issues. Orientation and focus are two prerequisites for productivity and high performance. If the manager takes the time to explain the reasons behind the questions, and explain how the answers will be used to make decisions, this has the added benefit of providing learning opportunities for subordinates. An important step in becoming an effective manager or leader is knowing how to ask responsible questions to collect information that will matter to the business.

HANDLING UNKNOWNS

Decisions are always about the future and facts are always about the past. The future and facts are mutually exclusive. Arthur W. Radford, US Navy Admiral, once said, "A decision is an action you must take when you have information so incomplete that the answer does not suggest itself." We can only make educated guesses and assumptions about the future.

Therefore, we have to take uncertainty into account and be aware of:

- what we know
- the limit of what we know
- what we don't know.

You might ask, "But what about statistical analysis? That's a pretty solid and factual way of making assumptions about the future, isn't it?" And yes, it's true that statistical analyses are based on facts and that they can be used to project the future. However, when it comes to social sciences and human behavior, they should only be used as a reference, not as the basis for decisions. In these areas, statistics are no substitute for human judgment.

To sum up: the future is full of uncertainties and unknowns. There are two kinds:

- **Knowable unknowns**—things we could know given enough resources (including time)
- **Unknowable unknowns**—things that we could never predict no matter how many resources we have, such as earthquakes and other "acts of God."

I suggest three ways of handling unknowns:

1. Turn the knowable unknowns into knowns.
2. Turn unknowns into potential risks, and manage them.
3. Choose reversible alternatives.

We'll look at each of these options now in a little more detail.

Turning knowable unknowns into knowns

We can allocate resources to turn knowable unknowns into knowns—do test runs, simulations, targeted pilots, and experiments. For instance, say we don't know how our target customers

We can allocate resources to turn knowable unknowns into knowns—do test runs, simulations, targeted pilots, and experiments

will react to a new product. The sensible thing to do is to introduce the new product into a few representative markets to test customer reactions, by launching focused trials and pilots in different regions to gather feedback and measure results. This uses few resources and allows us to adjust our product if necessary before its full-scale rollout.

Note that the resources we spend doing this should be in proportion to the degree of uncertainty and associated risk we face. The higher the degree of uncertainty and risk, the more we should spend. Also note that keeping accurate records of all experiments and tests is very important—without good data, we have wasted our experiments and the resources spent on them.

In 1999, I was responsible for IBM's Year 2000 Millennium (Y2K) project in the Asia-Pacific region. This was a new challenge, and because of the high degree of unknowns and risks involved, most people would not have chosen to be involved in the project at all, let alone to take on the Chief Information Officer (CIO) role. However, fear of the unknown does not help us to deal with it. As Edward H. Harriman, US financier and railroad magnate, said, "It's never safe to look into the future with eyes of fear."

We had to turn knowable unknowns into knowns. So we put all computer applications through test runs and simulations of the millennium crossover, measured the outcomes and made corrections. Then, we put all parts that had any electronic components through another crossover simulation, measured the outcomes and made corrections. Finally, we considered risks triggered by external factors—could we carry on if electricity supplies and telecommunication networks failed? We tested our risk management plans and crisis management plans.

We need to face the unknown and prepare for it. Listen to these words from Canadian publisher, R. I. Fitzhenry: "Uncertainty and mystery are energies of life. Don't let them scare you unduly, for they keep boredom at bay and spark creativity."

Convert unknowns into potential risks and manage them

We cannot control unknowns, but we can control risks, and prepare a crisis management plan if appropriate. Responsible managers should thus turn unknowns into potential risks and manage those risks.

With proper risk management and a crisis management plan, instead of fearing the unknown future, we can face it with open eyes. And as Thomas Fuller, English churchman and historian, said, "He that fears not the future may enjoy the present." Management will not be held accountable for "acts of God" (just as no insurance company will insure against them); management is only responsible for allocating adequate resources to deal with risks. For example, the management of an amusement park should test a roller-coaster ride thoroughly before opening it to the public. However, even with this thorough testing, the managers still need to consider any potential risks that are unrelated to the roller-coaster equipment, and manage those risks. For example, a passenger with a heart condition may not be able to cope with the excitement of the roller-coaster—so the managers must take measures to minimize or eliminate this risk (such as posting a warning that the ride is not suitable for people with heart conditions). They should also prepare a crisis management plan in case the preventative measures they have taken are not effective.

To go back to my Y2K example, the year 1999 was, for me, one of handling unknowns, managing risks, preparing for crises, and constantly reprioritizing. There were many unknowns and many more known risks, but our resources were finite. In particular, time was limited, as the deadline could not be moved. We could allocate more money to the Y2K project, but we could not slow the approach of January 1, 2000. Therefore, we had to prioritize our risk management actions according to their degree of uncertainty and associated risk.

For example, we tested how a model of office elevator would respond during the crossover—turning an unknown into a known. We then could ascertain the degree of risk involved and decide when to fix the elevators based on how that risk compared to other known risks, such as the failure of computer programs or machines at manufacturing sites. The risks with the biggest impacts were addressed first.

I want to highlight here that if you do not face the sort of time constraints we had on the Y2K project, phasing in changes is generally better than doing a full-scale simultaneous rollout. Even if you're relatively certain about the future, a phased approach allows you to manage risks better and make continuous improvements along the way, thus achieving a better total outcome.

Choosing reversible alternatives

If we face unknowns and risks that we cannot obtain enough resources to manage, then we need to choose "reversible alternatives." Some alternatives are inherently not reversible, such as giving birth to a child. Most, however, can be made reversible if we do so in advance of our final decision. To use some of our earlier case studies as examples:

- we could give Ms. Marsh a probationary period and specific milestones against which to measure success
- Tanaka Komuten could sign a collaboration agreement with Atlas that had "cancel without penalty" clauses under certain conditions
- Leclerc could create a new agreement with Creative, under which Leclerc would only spend the resources to protect Creative's sole distributorship if Creative achieved a certain minimum sales volume.

To put it another way, when there are many unknowns or the risk is high, we must give ourselves an exit strategy before we make the final decision. And if there are multiple alternatives with a similar value, but some are reversible and some are irreversible, then we should choose the reversible ones—even if we are fairly certain about the outcomes. If you do decide to choose an irreversible alternative, make sure you can live with the worst-case scenario. As quoted in Chapter 6, "If you can take the worst, take the risk."

I must stress again, however, that "take the risk" should mean "dare to experiment responsibly", not "gamble irresponsibly". If we gamble, we will most likely suffer negative consequences sooner or later. By contrast, if we dare to experiment innovatively, using conscious risk management, we will certainly achieve better outcomes step by step. Our cumulative improvements will be difficult to beat.

ONGOING COURSE CORRECTION

As we mentioned earlier, acquiring the information we need to make decisions involves establishing checkpoints at which to evaluate our decisions in the future. Information must be collected to serve two purposes:

1. To monitor and validate our assumptions. For example, say we assume GDP will grow 5 percent over the next year and allocate resources based on this assumption. If actual GDP growth is only 3 percent, we must adjust our decision (our resource allocation) to bring about better outcomes. It's never a good idea to wait for the situation to force a change.

2. To measure our progress toward our goals. All decisions are made to achieve specific goals: are we progressing toward them with the expected speed? If the answer is yes, our team deserves positive recognition. If not, find out why and adjust the decision to ensure a better outcome.

COMMON FAILURES IN INFORMATION

There are a number of common failures in respect to gathering and using information:

- Focusing on the past information that's available, not on what information will be needed in the future
- Neglecting to obtain important information that can help us to make the next decision
- Basing decisions entirely on statistics and survey results
- Collecting half-truths and missing the interdependencies or facts that show us causes and effects—the total picture

- Using available information instead of relevant and valid information
- Focusing on what we know, not on what's important
- Focusing only on what we know, and ignoring what we don't know or the limit of what we know

As we make each decision, we should make sure we can answer the following three questions in detail:

- What information is needed to help us to make the next decision?
- How do we acquire this information?
- How do we use the information, once acquired?

If you cannot answer these questions explicitly and comprehensively, you may be wasting resources by collecting the information.

CASE STUDY

The situation: AlwaysOpen

Mr. Michael Sampson and Mr. Kevin Bennett, the CEO and CFO of the convenience store chain AlwaysOpen, need to decide whether to abandon their unique Aviva strategy. Two years ago, AlwaysOpen adopted this new strategy in the hope of differentiating itself from competing convenience stores. It aimed to attract middle-class, middle-aged people by providing a relaxed and entertaining in-store atmosphere based on themes and promotions. However, they have just received a market research report for the second half of the year, indicating that the Aviva strategy is not resonating with customers. The report states that on a scale of one to 10, AlwaysOpen scored only 5.44 for the characteristic "Being a relaxed or entertaining place." In fact, this characteristic received the lowest score of all the characteristics surveyed. The highest two characteristics, scoring 7.1 and 7.09 respectively, were "Cleanliness and neatness" and "Friendliness of staff." Clearly, customers have not picked up on the Aviva strategy.

AlwaysOpen's financial performance, however, has steadily improved in the last two years. Operating profit was higher in the low-season months this year than it was in the high-season months two years ago. AlwaysOpen has a balanced scorecard showing improvement in all financial measures, customer measures, internal measures, and even learning and growth measures. Both managers and crewmembers have improved their skills significantly. But there is no data on the customers—no contact details, no information on their income, age, the products they purchase, their in-store spending, how often they visit, and so on.

Dialogue: Can we trust the data?

Characters: Mr. Michael Sampson, CEO of AlwaysOpen
Mr. Kevin Bennett, CFO of AlwaysOpen

Mr. Sampson and Mr. Bennett are discussing what they should do about the market research report.

Sampson: Well, Kevin, what should we make of this data? Can we trust this market research? What do you think?

Bennett: We also need to consider if the problem is with our strategy or if it is just our implementation. What does that market research report say again?

Sampson: On the most recent customer surveys, it says that there is low differentiation of AlwaysOpen from our competitors. The customers just aren't picking up the relaxed, enjoyable shopping experience we were trying to create with our Aviva campaign. The survey results say that our customers value fast service and good product selection. Can we rely on that? Does this mean that we don't need a relaxed in-store atmosphere as long as we have fast service and a wide range of product selections? And you're right, we need to know if the problem is in the implementation of the Aviva campaign, or if the whole strategy was flawed to begin with.

Bennett: Well, Michael, some store sales only grew by the industry average of 6 percent. The customer complaint box always contains some complaints about the Aviva campaign, but that doesn't necessarily mean anything, because people are more apt to complain than to praise. On the other hand, our customer focus groups did show that our customers value good product selection, quick service, and clean surroundings. They were not too interested in the Aviva experience that we were trying to create.

Discussion

After two years, AlwaysOpen's management team is still puzzled about whether the Aviva strategy has been successful or not. All the data they have, including the elaborate balanced scorecard, cannot answer this basic question.

Sampson and Bennett should have chosen measures of success when they made the decision to go with the Aviva strategy, and started collecting information that would allow the decision to be evaluated and adjusted in the future. Remember our two course-correction purposes?

1. To monitor and validate our assumptions
2. To measure our progress toward our goals

They should first have asked themselves, "What assumptions did we make about the future that led to our decision to implement the Aviva strategy?" Was it an increase of middle-class, middle-aged people in the population? An increase in that segment's disposable income? An increased preference among this group for shopping at convenience stores? A preference among this group for a relaxed, entertaining shopping atmosphere?

Then, what was the supporting information for these assumptions when they were made? That information should have been checked at appropriate intervals after the Aviva campaign began. Statistics on population, disposable income, and shopping preferences do not usually change much on a daily, weekly, or monthly basis, so a quarterly or semi-annual check of this data may have been sufficient. If the current information no longer supported their previous assumptions, they should have re-examined the decision and made adjustments to obtain a better outcome.

Next, what about goals? What were the objectives of Aviva? What were the measures of success and milestones? Did they aim, for example, for the visits of middle-class, middle-aged people to AlwaysOpen stores to increase by 20 percent in six months? To increase sales revenue from this market segment? To increase profits? To increase market share for AlwaysOpen overall? To improve brand image among this segment of population? To increase customer satisfaction? To increase customer loyalty, shown through repeat visits and purchases?

Did they progress toward those goals at the expected speed? If yes, then Aviva is successful; if no, then Aviva is not successful enough. Aviva was an experiment, and if they did not define success and did not measure its progress, it is a wasted experiment.

We must have the means of collecting the information we need. How could AlwaysOpen have tracked the visits of middle-class, middle-aged people to their stores and recorded their purchases? Also, we must know how we are going to use the information we collect. For example, would Sampson and Bennett have used the information on Aviva to decide whether to continue the campaign or not? Or would they have used it to evaluate the performance of the staff involved in implementing the strategy? If we cannot answer such questions logically and in detail, why are we spending resources to collect the information? Keep in mind, too, that the cost of collecting information should not exceed the benefits it will bring.

Let's recap the three questions we need to ask before gathering information. They were:

1. What information is needed to help us make the next decision?
2. How can we acquire this information?
3. How can we use this information once acquired?

It may not be easy to answer these questions explicitly and in detail, but it is essential in order to make quality decisions and achieve good outcomes.

Now that we understand objective reasoning and the basics of gathering the information we need to make quality decisions, let's turn to the final component of IPO—the people involved in the decision-making process.

CHAPTER 8

IPO: P for People

The last component for a quality decision-making process is people. All decisions—no matter how good or bad, right or wrong—are made by people; therefore, people are of utmost importance. High-quality decision making requires the following three types of people to participate in or support the process:

- **Decision makers**—people who are willing and able to allocate resources so that decisions can be implemented
- **Supporters**—people who must support the decisions in order for them to be successfully implemented
- **Participants**—people who need to participate in the decision-making process in order to increase the quality of the decisions

Only decision makers are fully involved in the entire decision-making process. Supporters do not necessarily need to participate in the decision-making meetings, but must support the final decision in order for it to be implementable. Participants need to participate in the decision-making process to increase the quality of the final decision, but their consent is not mandatory to it. We'll now look at these three groups in turn.

DECISION MAKERS

Decision makers are those who are willing and able to allocate resources. However, they do not necessarily own those resources or acquire them—although if they do, the decision-making process is more straightforward. Sometimes leaders delegate the task of allocating resources to others, as all their available time is spent acquiring the resources. In this case, the leader becomes a supporter, and the people who actually allocate the resources become the decision makers.

There can be more than one decision maker in an organization, if the implementation of decisions requires resources to be allocated by multiple parties. However, there should be a primary decision maker who leads and coordinates the others and facilitates the decision-making process. Usually, this is either the person who will contribute the largest portion of resources or the one who cares most about the decision's consequences.

Before making each decision, and throughout the decision-making process, the decision maker must consciously involve the supporters and participants. In a quality decision-making process, these people cannot be neglected, as decisions cannot be executed successfully without them. Getting their support must be a forethought, not an afterthought. Without it, the decision might not be successfully implemented, even if it was made well, costing the decision maker his or her credibility.

Throughout the decision-making process, the decision maker must consciously involve supporters and participants

SUPPORTERS

Supporters often do not need to participate in the decision-making process: they simply need to buy into the final decision in order for it to be executed. The decision maker should thus stay in contact with the supporters before and throughout the decision-making process to retain their support.

There are two types of supporters:

1. Those who can support the decision and make it stick
2. Those who can veto the decision

The first type of supporters are usually people with superior intangible assets—those with higher social status, more "face," higher credibility, higher rank, or a higher position of power, for example. These supporters may not be able to allocate any tangible resources, but we may need their intangible resources in order to acquire tangible resources from other parties to make the decision. If our decision-making authority was delegated to us by someone else, then that person is this type of supporter. Or perhaps, if our decision involves significant changes, we simply need these people's moral support to help us, personally, persist through the changes.

When a decision involves innovation and change, it is good to ask ourselves before we begin the decision-making process, "If the rest of the world opposed my final decision, whose endorsement would I need in order to persist boldly through my change management cycle?" That person or group of people are our supporters, and we need them with us from the start, even though they may not participate in the decision-making meetings and discussions. They must be kept informed and we must know for sure that we have their support all along the way. They usually will not give their support if we just inform them of our decision after making it, or if we ask them when we are struggling with the implementation of a decision they have had nothing to do with.

The second type of supporters cannot make decisions stick, but they are in a position to veto them. In other words, their "yes" alone is relatively unimportant, but their "no" can shut us down. This type of supporter is usually someone in a regulatory role externally or internally. They may be from a government agency that issues permits, licenses, and governmental approvals; or they may be from our organization's human resources, legal, or internal audit departments. If we don't have their support, we cannot implement our decision, even if it is perfect.

For instance, let's suppose that I am a sales manager. By the end of the year, I realize my sales numbers have almost met my target—I just need my salespeople to work a little harder. I decide to set up a reward system to motivate my salespeople, as I have the budget. However, someone may emerge to stop my plan. Perhaps someone from the human resources (HR) department thinks my reward system is unfair to others in the organization. The HR person cannot help me to reach my sales target, but he or she can veto my motivational tools and prevent me from meeting the target in that way. Therefore, I need to get HR support before and throughout the decision-making process in order to implement the decision.

PARTICIPANTS

Participants are people who can improve the quality and implementation of a decision. It's important that they participate in the decision-making process, especially when alternatives are being generated and during the objective reasoning phase. Participants cannot veto the final decision, but their participation will ensure its quality. (If some participants' support is mandatory for the final decision, then they are also supporters.)

In addition to our own team members, some of the participants in our alternative-generation process could be carefully chosen outsiders; for example, external consultants. These must be knowledgeable and credible, and must not have any conflict of interest or any vested interest in the decision—then they are free to challenge our thinking, to help us jump out of our "well" and see a different or broader perspective, and to provide innovative alternatives. The value of outsiders to innovation should not be ignored. However, their ideas may be too impractical to implement in our environment. So, we also need a different kind of participant during the objective reasoning phase to help us select the best alternative.

As I mentioned in Chapter 6, participants in the objective reasoning phase should have "been there, done that." They should be experienced and understand the potential consequences of the alternatives we have come up with. Be aware, however, that their past experience may have made them more conservative, biased, or risk-averse; they usually like to collect data to reinforce the validity of their previous experiences. They are unlikely to innovate, so they are not the kind of person who can help us with generating creative ideas, but we need them to help us anticipate potential problems and risks associated with our alternatives and choose the alternatives that have the highest odds of successful implementation. They may be internal or external to our organization, but are generally older and wiser people, and are able to suggest practical methods of managing risks and preventing negative consequences. So they are good advisors during the objective reasoning stage.

For example, if we are thinking of expanding through mergers and acquisitions (M&As), we may need external parties to help us generate M&A alternatives. Then, we need to involve different parties to help us think, during the process of selecting the best alternative, about post-M&A integration. The participation of both of these groups of parties during the generation and selection of M&A alternatives can help us to increase the quality of our final decision. However, they cannot make the decision for us, nor can they veto our decision.

Throughout the decision-making process, only decision makers, supporters, and participants should be involved. No other people can contribute to the quality of our decision—they can only potentially slow down the decision-making process. We therefore need to do our best to exclude such bystanders from decision-making discussions.

We have to stress the importance of sharing and contribution throughout the process. Team members should be encouraged to contribute innovative alternatives and participate in objective reasoning, because they have to implement the decision made. Participation will also get their "buy-in" and make them aware in advance of a decision's potential positive and negative consequences. In this way, the entire team can be well-prepared for its implementation.

COMMON FAILURES REGARDING PEOPLE

The five most common failings of decision makers with regard to the people involved in the decision-making process are as follows:

1. Not ensuring all parties involved are clear about goals and priorities
2. Involving irrelevant people who do not add value and slow down the process
3. Not obtaining buy-in from supporters before and during the process
4. Not providing avenues for team members to participate and contribute
5. Using inappropriate leadership styles during various phases of process

The first four of these points we have discussed already; the last one, relating to leadership styles, we will explore in the next section.

LEADERSHIP STYLES

In the decision-making process, an effective leader needs to use multiple leadership styles. There are a lot of books and theories about the art of leadership; however, I like things simple, so for the purposes of this section I have chosen to use the six leadership styles listed by Daniel Goleman in his "Leadership that Gets Results" article in the *Harvard Business Review* (March 2000). The styles are:

- Coercive (Do what I tell you)
- Authoritative (Come with me)
- Affiliative (People come first)
- Democratic (What do you think?)
- Pace setting (Do as I do, now)
- Coaching (Try this)

Do not confuse leadership styles with personalities—your personality is consistent and innate; a leadership style should be situational.

I liken leadership styles to colors. When we look at one color at a time, there is no right or wrong, no good or bad. However, when multiple colors are put together, an effect is created—a particular combination may seem "orderly" or "chaotic," "hot" or "cool," "light" or "dark." The same color put with other colors will create very different effects. In the same way, a leader who only has one leadership style will find that his or her "single color" may work well with a certain set of people and situations. But when those people and situations change, if the leader cannot alter leadership style, he or she cannot be effective.

Let me illustrate: say that someone you know likes to wear red. Every time she dresses in red, people say she looks good. So red clothing becomes her trademark—because of people's compliments, she always wears red. But there may come a day when a red outfit is not appropriate. Someone says to her, "We really like you, but red clothes are not suitable for this occasion. Could you please wear another color?" If she is unwilling to change, or unable to change because her wardrobe now only has red clothes, she may not be able to attend the event.

Matching leadership style to situation

There is no right or wrong in the matter of leadership style; we can only evaluate leadership styles by their effectiveness: What combination of leadership styles will be effective for the task at hand? Will our leadership style be effective with the people we need to lead in our current situation? Will our leadership style allow us to effectively carry out our responsibility to achieve the organization's shared goal?

Everyone has a style which is most natural to him or her, but effective leaders pay attention to the overall effect produced by a combination of different styles (colors). An effective leader is willing and able to adjust his or her own styles according to the needs of time, place, and people, in order to produce the most desirable

There is a time and place for everything, but nothing is good for all times and places

outcome. There is a time and place for everything, but nothing is good for all times and places.

To give the most obvious example: the most effective leadership style for leading a team to make decisions in normal business circumstances may not be effective during emergencies. (Of course, if we always lead the team to make the best use of our finite resources to progress toward the goal, and employ sound risk management, then there should be very few emergencies. If we manage our risk well, we will seldom need to activate our crisis management plan.)

Lastly, it is worth noting that leaders should use the same leadership style to deal with the same kind of people in the same circumstances. If they fail to do this, they are not being consistent or fair, and their credibility will suffer.

Effective decision-making leadership styles

In my experience, the most effective leadership styles, using Goleman's terms, are as follows for each dimension of the GPA IPO decision-making framework:

- Goal—authoritative
- Priorities—authoritative plus democratic
- Alternatives—democratic
- Objective reasoning—coaching
- Information—coaching
- People—affiliative

The goal

For the goal dimension, an authoritative style is the most effective. If a leader cannot tell the team members to "Come with me" towards a clear, motivating and shared goal, how can he or she lead the team to achieve that goal? The leader has to keep the goal in view at all times and communicate it to the team members clearly, specifically, and frequently. He or she must be confident, leading the team with a passionate sense of mission, motivating team members to pursue the shared goal, and mobilizing them to make their vision a reality.

Priorities

For the priorities aspect, authoritative and democratic styles should be used. If you remember, to set priorities we need two data points: the desired future state (the goal) and the current state. The leader must have a vision of the desired future state, but he or she may not have a deep understanding of the details of the current state. Therefore, leaders often have to consult the team members democratically about the current conditions both internally and in the marketplace—the current state of business.

After gaps are identified, then comes the difficult task of prioritization: "What's the most important thing to address next?" The team needs to prioritize the shorter-term objectives and sequence tasks in order to reach the long-term goal. They also need to ensure that the current state remains above the baseline. This is difficult, because it involves real trade-offs and give and take. Therefore, after the leader receives democratic input about current conditions, he or she can be authoritative in laying out the priorities and identifying the most important milestones for the next stage. The leader also needs to be authoritative in allocating adequate resources to protect the baseline, which is not negotiable.

Alternatives

When generating alternatives, the democratic style must be used—we will not have a creative and proactive team otherwise. A democratic style stresses equal participation, contribution, and open communication among team members. The generation of new ideas by all team members should be encouraged to become a normal, everyday practice, and input from team members should always be welcomed and considered. Think about it: if we hire talented people and then do not provide them with a platform for contributing ideas and using their talents, it will be a total waste of precious human resources.

Through conscious cultivation and practice over a period of time, innovation can become the culture, the habit, of the team. Consistently encourage innovation, allocate resources for experiments, allow failures—but demand progress! Never stop looking for better alternatives.

Objective reasoning

The objective reasoning stage works best with a coaching style of leadership. The leader guides the team to think about the consequences of each alternative and what resources are needed to realize the organization's shared dream while preventing nightmares. This kind of coaching can help the team members to take ownership during implementation, and to be prepared for the consequences.

We can objectively coach a team by asking relevant questions:

- What resources are needed to implement this alternative successfully?
- Will the consequences of this alternative bring us closer to the goal? At what speed?
- What difficulties and challenges will we face if this alternative is implemented?
- How will we handle the risks associated with the implementation of this alternative? Are there ways to prevent, eliminate, reduce, dilute, or diversify the risks?
- What resources are needed to implement our risk management plan?
- Do we know where the resources are coming from and where they are going?

The focus should not be on who's right or wrong, but on how resources can be best allocated to achieve the shared goal and reduce risks.

Information

The information dimension works best with a coaching style of leadership: the leader guides the team to think about how to measure their success in the future. This kind of coaching can help team members to anticipate their responsibilities during implementation, and understand performance expectations.

We can objectively coach a team in this area by asking various questions:

- What are the measures of success for this decision?
- What information do we need to collect in order to measure our success and make timely adjustments?
- What are the data sources and formats required?
- How do we collect this information, and how frequently should it be collected?
- How are we going to use the information—in what management reports will we use it and for what managerial purpose?
- What resources are needed to collect and use our information?

The focus of data collection should not be on satisfying everyone's slightest curiosity, but on using the information to help us make timely adjustments, in order to achieve the best outcome for our decisions.

The people

An affiliative style of leadership should be used with people. If we invite someone to be involved in our decision-making process, that person must be a decision maker, a supporter, or a participant. We should always pay respect to these people when asking for their input and contribution.

CASE STUDY

The situation: Hanover Public Systems

Hanover Public Systems (HPS) is a US manufacturer of industrial electrical equipment, including elevators, lighting systems, heating and cooling equipment, and industrial fans. The company began to establish foreign manufacturing subsidiaries two decades ago; at present, it has eight wholly-owned subsidiaries abroad in addition to its four large domestic plants. The financial performance of the foreign subsidiaries has been good, with the exception of the China facility, which has been losing money at a precipitous rate for the past three years.

In the mid-year report, the HPS Beijing office reported further substantial losses, despite an infusion of US$3 million from the parent company earlier in the year. After considerable study and deliberation, the president of the Chinese plant, Mr. Yang, was fired and replaced with Mr. James Fukuda, a second-generation Japanese-American who was formerly vice president of operations at the Oakland, California plant. At 38, Mr. Fukuda is the youngest person ever to become an HPS president. He is regarded by head office in New York as a brilliant manager, as he initiated policies during his three-year tenure in Oakland—including a much-needed managerial reorganization—that resulted in phenomenal growth. In the opinion of head office, he was clearly the best person to take over the ailing subsidiary.

Upon being named president, and even before arriving in Beijing, Mr. Fukuda began to make changes. His first action was to dispose of some of the subsidiary's assets and inventory to pay down liabilities—a course that had been rejected by his predecessor, Mr. Yang. His second action, after just one week in Beijing, was to cease the manufacturing of heating and cooling equipment—a decision totally opposed by the all-Chinese staff at HPS China. This action resulted in the lay-off of 18 workers and the reassignment of 12 more, and drew considerable heat from the staff.

Fukuda's third action, after just a month on the job, was to employ a totally new management system. This decision outraged the HPS China executives to the point that both the vice president of operations (Mr. Hu) and the plant superintendent (Mr. Zhang) resigned. Led by Mr. Lo, the executive director of finance, 14 middle-level and upper-level managers sent a letter (which is shown following) to HPS president, Mr. Howard Wolff, expressing their dismay and questioning Mr. Fukuda's policies. Wolff had conceived and established HPS China himself and had worked closely with a number of the letter's signatories. He began to wonder if Mr. Fukuda was maybe moving a little too fast.

Letter from Mr. Lo to Mr. Wolff

HPS China
A Subsidiary of Hanover Public Systems, Inc.
Beijing, People's Republic of China

Mr. Howard Wolff
President
Hanover Public Systems
New York, N.Y. 10020

Dear Mr. Wolff,

We, the middle- and upper-level managers at HPS China, are writing to you as a last resort. As you are well aware, the financial situation at our company has necessitated a number of changes designed to increase our profitability. Among the measures instituted by President Fukuda are partial liquidation, cessation of manufacturing heating and cooling systems, and managerial reorganization. While we understand the need for sweeping changes for cost-effective reasons, we take issue with two of Mr. Fukuda's actions—his decision to halt production of heating and cooling systems, and his reorganization plan.

Although none of us would argue that heating and cooling systems have been profitable during the last two years, Mr. Fukuda's action does not take into consideration a number of factors. One, the decline in sales has been due chiefly to artificially low prices set by our competition (mainly Japanese manufacturers) in an attempt to drive us out of the market. It is clear that their profit margin (if any) is small and therefore cannot continue, nor are their prices indicative of the fair market value of the product. If we were to lower our prices substantially, we too could compete in this current price war. Two, Mr. Fukuda is ignoring the hardships placed on laid-off and reassigned workers. Within the factory, these lay-offs have resulted in depressed morale among the workers on their assembly lines. Surely, halting production of these systems is not the only viable solution available to him?

The other matter that concerns us is Mr. Fukuda's American-style (or Japanese-style) reorganization plan. In our collective opinion, it is extremely unwise. There are three main problems with it. First, it consolidates sales into one division. Although this may be more immediately cost-effective, in the long run it may seriously affect the reputation and sales of HPS China, since sales of our equipment are dependent upon our sales force having a specialized knowledge of the product they are selling. Under Mr. Fukuda's plan, salespeople will sell all Hanover products, even those that they are not familiar with, a situation that could backfire if the product sold is not appropriate to the client's needs.

Second, Mr. Fukuda has so far not designated who will be in charge of what division after the reorganization. He claims he "wants to see us in action" before he makes a decision. This creates unfair anxiety among all of us, since we do not know whether we are to be promoted, demoted, or even fired.

Third, Mr. Fukuda has created this plan without consulting us and without having any knowledge of the intricacies of doing business in China. Since we are all native Chinese with years of accumulated business experience, we deeply resent his manner of dealing. This lack of regard for those of us who have served the company proudly has already resulted in the resignations of Mr. Hu and Mr. Zhang, two able and expert managers.

We are sorry to have to bring this matter to your attention, but we have been unable to talk with Mr. Fukuda about it. We also feel that the situation has become so serious that it is imperative that you, whom we have always trusted as a sincere and sensitive man, know about it. We thank you for your time and attention to our plea.

Sincerely yours,
C. Lo
Executive Director, Finance Division
(and 13 others)

Dialogue: A leadership style discussion

Characters: Mr. Howard Wolff, HPS President
Mr. James Fukuda, President, HPS China

Mr. Fukuda has just been informed by his secretary that Mr. Wolff is on the line from New York.

Fukuda:	Howard?
Wolff:	Jim, how are you?
Fukuda:	Good thanks. What's up?
Wolff:	Well, I'm calling for a couple of reasons. I'll get the minor matters out of the way first. I need a complete inventory update a.s.a.p.
Fukuda:	Okay. Next.
Wolff:	Jim, I trust you got a copy of the letter sent to me by Mr. Hu and Mr. Zhang after their resignations.
Fukuda:	Yeah, I saw it.
Wolff:	It's too bad we had to lose Hu and Zhang. They were good people.
Fukuda:	I was surprised myself at their resignations. But I guess they felt they had to do it to save face.
Wolff:	You couldn't persuade them otherwise?
Fukuda:	They didn't give me much of a chance. They obviously had their minds made up.
Wolff:	I see. Well, how are things there now?
Fukuda:	To be honest, Howard, it's tough going. In fact, I've got something of a rebellion on my hands at the moment. It'll pass soon, though. Once the managers realize that the changes I want to make are for their own good, I think we'll see some real changes in attitude.
Wolff:	That may be true, but they're upset now, and I'm not sure we can afford that. Morale hasn't been so hot for some time there, and it seems we've gone from bad to worse. And that's counterproductive to anything we might want to do in terms of recovery.
Fukuda:	But, Howard, that's to be expected. Give it some time. The point is we can't wait for people to be happy with every decision to initiate some new measures here. As you know, Yang pleased everybody in this subsidiary for years while driving it to the point of bankruptcy. I'm not interested in alienating the people that I have to work with, but at the same time I'm not trying to win any popularity awards either. Certain measures had to be taken and taken immediately. I took them. And already we have current assets in excess of current liabilities.

Wolff:	Jim, I know, and I'm not questioning your fiscal policies. I am wondering, though, if maybe you could hold off a bit on the reorganization. My personal feeling is that with all the other changes going on this is not the best thing to take on right now. When you reorganized in Oakland, it worked fine because the operation itself was sound and because you were not perceived by middle management as an outsider. But you're in China, Jim, not Oakland. And that matters.
Fukuda:	I know I'm in China, and I know that I'm resented because I'm not Chinese. At the same time, I'm doing what I feel I have to do to save this subsidiary. And a reshuffle is one of those measures.
Wolff:	But, Jim, you're not running China by yourself. You're making the key decisions, sure, and that's what we expect you to do, but you've got to have cooperation if those decisions are to be implemented.
Fukuda:	I'm well aware of that. I admit I may have moved a little too fast with reorganization. But one of the main problems here is the organization. It's got to be dealt with. They'll come around. Right now, everybody's on edge—threatened, worried. Also, because I'm Japanese-American it's worse.
Wolff:	What does that have to do with it?
Fukuda:	The Chinese don't like the Japanese. History, you know.
Wolff:	Oh, come on.
Fukuda:	I'm serious.
Wolff:	Well, nobody there is bringing that up.
Fukuda:	Not to you, maybe, but I can feel it. Anyway, it doesn't matter. What matters is that we're making progress. And you'll see, as we start to make a profit again, the attitudes will change.
Wolff:	I just hope that you're right and that the attitudes won't get in the way of making a profit. Do make an effort to communicate, though. It's vital. Talk it out with them. Get their advice. They know and care a lot about the business.

Discussion

From the conversation between Mr. Fukuda and Mr. Wolff, we can tell that Mr. Fukuda felt he was carrying out the company's mission to return HPS

China to profitability, and therefore, he was bold even when faced with a significant internal morale problem. Mr. Fukuda felt that if the China business had been running well, the company would not have sent him to China in the first place. He also thought that if the Chinese team had been capable of high performance, the China business would have been profitable. Thus, he felt justified in taking drastic actions to turn the business around quickly. Staff dissatisfaction was predictable and understandable.

From Mr. Wolff's perspective, he had made the decision to send Mr. Fukuda to China because he considered him the best alternative to achieve the goal of turning around the business there. Now, the information Wolff has received is making him wonder whether his decision was a good one.

Mr. Wolff's decision was based on the assumption that Mr. Fukuda was willing and able to handle the business in China—now it appears that that assumption is not entirely correct. At very least, Mr. Fukuda has not demonstrated enough sensitivity in a cross-cultural environment, which calls into question his ability to lead changes in a cross-cultural environment. There is room for improvement in him. So, Mr. Wolff needs to make some adjustments to his previous decision in order to get the best outcome.

What adjustment should he make? It depends on what the gap is between the goal and the current state. Obviously, there was a performance gap in HPS China that is being closed due to Mr. Fukuda's actions. But now there is a gap regarding Mr. Fukuda's leadership and management style that may hinder him from leading his Chinese team to sustained success. If we look at our list of the leadership styles that are desirable for the various dimensions of the GPA IPO framework, we can see the following:

1. The **goal**—Mr. Fukuda did not communicate his goals well enough to the Chinese employees. He may have assumed that everyone knew them, but in any case, he failed to say, "Come with me" authoritatively, clearly, specifically, and repeatedly. So Mr. Fukuda's Chinese management team did not follow him, and they probably wondered about Mr. Fukuda's personal agenda and where he was leading the company.

2. **Priorities**—In order to prioritize, Mr. Fukuda, who is new to China, needs two sets of data: the current state and the future desired

state. He may be very clear in his own mind about the future state, but he needs to use the democratic and consultative style to gain a deep understanding of the current state from his Chinese management team. If he did this, his team could implement his priorities with conviction.

3. **Alternatives**—Mr. Fukuda failed to democratically involve his team in generating multiple innovative alternatives. As said before, he seems to have felt that if the Chinese management had had good ideas, the business in China would have been better and the company would not have appointed him. He may be right, but he cannot be certain until he has given his team opportunities to participate and contribute. By not giving his team these opportunities, he has wasted precious human resources and alienated his team.

4. **Objective reasoning**—Mr. Fukuda also failed to involve his team in objective reasoning to choose the best alternative according to its consequences. Therefore, the team questioned his judgment, and became concerned about the impact his arbitrary actions would have on the subsidiary's future.

   The alternatives and objective reasoning stages give Mr. Fukuda the opportunity to observe the willingness and ability of each team member, so he can learn their strengths and weaknesses. Then, he will be able to place each member of his team in the appropriate role in his new managerial structure to maximize the benefit from their strengths; he will be able to coach team members more effectively in the future.

5. **People**—Mr. Wolff delegated authority to Mr. Fukuda regarding HPS China; therefore, he is one of Mr. Fukuda's supporters. Mr. Fukuda should have used the affiliative style to keep in touch with him and retain his support throughout the decision-making process. Mr. Wolff does not need to participate in the process, but he must support the decisions in order for Mr. Fukuda to implement them successfully.

   During the alternatives and objective reasoning stages, some appropriate outside advisors or consultants from China and US headquarters should have participated as well as the Chinese management team. By involving people with diverse backgrounds and experiences, more innovative ideas could have been generated and the team would have been better prepared for the final decision and its implementation.

Mr. Wolff also needs to exercise caution in his handling of the conflicts between Mr. Fukuda and his Chinese team. His focus should not be on judging which side is right and which wrong, as from the other side of the world he cannot get the most current and complete facts. Remember—half-truths can be misleading. If Mr. Wolff takes a side, he destroys the second prerequisite for teamwork: interdependence. Mr. Fukuda and his team will no longer need to depend on one another to succeed in China; they will only need to depend on Mr. Wolff, as whoever can get support from the boss will win. The company boss should only be on the side of the shared goal, and must not pit team members against one another or tacitly promote office politics. Each member must be evaluated solely by how they contribute to the team and to its progress toward the shared goal.

Also, since history cannot be changed, Mr. Wolff should encourage the team to forget the past and work together for their shared goal in the future. He should coach Mr. Fukuda to communicate clearly, specifically, and repeatedly about the goal with his team. He might even advise that Mr. Fukuda establish a suggestion-award system so that his team will proactively pursue the goal together.

Mr. Wolff could, in addition, thank Mr. Fukuda for his past efforts and give him clear expectations regarding his performance in the future. That is, in addition to financial improvement, Mr. Fukuda needs to demonstrate he can lead a cross-cultural team to higher performance. If Mr. Fukuda can, he will step up to this clearly expressed higher expectation. If he fails to meet the expectation, Mr. Wolff can arrange a different job for him in the future.

In any case, no change should be made right after the letter from Mr. Lo, or Mr. Lo will get the impression that he has "won" against Mr. Fukuda. Mr. Wolff should demand that both Mr. Fukuda and Mr. Lo step up to higher performance by pursuing the shared goal together. They should not be compared to each other; rather, both should be evaluated by their contribution to the achievement of the shared goal, and by the teamwork and leadership they demonstrate in the process.

CHAPTER 9

Conclusion

The price of greatness is responsibility.

—Winston Churchill

Great leaders bear great responsibilities. While all leaders must be willing to take on the responsibilities that come with their role, those who are willing and able to take on greater responsibilities make greater leaders. And the most important responsibility of a leader is to make responsible, quality decisions.

Power comes with greatness, as well. I like Baroness Margaret Thatcher's words: "Being powerful is like being a lady. If you have to tell people you are, you aren't." Power, however, is granted to leaders in order for them to fulfill their responsibilities; it is not to be used for their own benefit. Leaders should make decisions to create value for all stakeholders and society as a whole, and to achieve the organizational goals that the team members share. Thus, leaders should have a decision-making framework that can be communicated to all members and practiced by all members, and that is open to public examination. A publicly shared decision-making framework can prevent endless unproductive debates. Team members should know that their constructive participation and contributions are needed to improve the quality of the decision; they should also know that they will share in the decision's consequences, because the alternative selected is the result of the team's collective innovative suggestions.

Many people have asked me why it is that, even though the GPA IPO framework is so simple and easy to understand, it is not habitually practiced. How can we ensure that we use the GPA IPO framework in all our decisions? Well, the answer is the same as for any new habit: Practice makes perfect. Having the discipline to practice is the key.

Here is what I have done to keep myself honestly practicing what I preach:

1. I used the power and diverse thinking of the whole team to make each decision better. I made my decision-making framework public, then authorized my team to challenge me and anyone else on the team if we forgot to use the framework or could not explain our decisions. I believe a single person is more likely to fall into a trap than a group of people, unless that group is very homogeneous—which may be another problem in itself. A team whose members have diverse backgrounds can certainly be more creative than a homogeneous team.

    It is better to put pressure on the entire team to produce innovative experiments than to put pressure on a specific individual. A group's objective reasoning will be more objective than an individual's, too. In my experience, when a team has a common decision-making framework that encourages diverse thinking and demands creative alternatives, a better decision can be made by the group than by any single person. The odds of the decision being successfully implemented by the team are also increased.

    In addition, a common decision-making framework will eliminate office politics, and it allows leaders to share the power of decision making without losing control, since the leader sets the goal and priorities and will be held accountable for the outcome

2. I started using this framework on routine daily decisions, such as how I should use my weekend time and how I should spend my monthly budget. Before shopping, I would ask myself, "What are my objectives and scope?" When I was influenced by an ad towards making a purchase, I would ask myself, "Is this the most important item on which to spend my finite resources? Will spending the same amount of money on another item generate a more positive impact? Have I covered my baseline adequately with time and money?"

    Start with small decisions and apply the decision-making framework frequently to build up the habit of using it. Repeated actions become habits, and the sum of our habits becomes our character. Once we build up the habit of using GPA IPO to approach any decision, we will become known for making responsible decisions—and we will be able to successfully implement our decisions by involving the right people in our decision-making process.

Remember, continuous improvement is a cycle comprised of three steps:

1. Observe
2. Think
3. Experiment

If perfection is the target, then progress is the indicator. We may not be able to demand perfection on every task every time, but we can demand progress on every task every time. And on the road to perfection, progress needs to be recognized and congratulated. This can motivate everyone to continue to observe, think and experiment to continuously improve.

During the decision-making process, we should frequently ask ourselves the following questions to assess the quality of a decision and to make timely improvements:

- Are we allocating enough resources to constantly observe and think about the changes around us, externally and internally?
- Do we need to reaffirm our goal?
- Is our goal long term and clearly defined? Is our goal clearly communicated and shared?
- Do we have clear objectives, a defined scope, and a conscious perspective regarding each resource allocation?
- Have adequate resources been allocated to cover our baseline?
- Are we clear about the gap between our current state and the goal? Are we closing the right gap?
- Have all tasks been prioritized by importance?
- Are we doing the most important thing first?
- Do we have many innovative alternatives for carrying out our priority tasks?
- Have we thought thoroughly about the consequences of all these alternatives?
- Did we choose the alternative that will have the best consequences?
- Do we have a risk management plan? (And a crisis management plan, if one is called for?)
- Have we defined the measure of success for this decision?
- Have appropriate resources been allocated to implement the decision and manage the risks? Where are these resources coming from and going to?
- Have resources been allocated to communicate the decision to all those who need to know and support the implementation?

- Have resources been allocated for us to collect information in order to measure our success and adjust our decisions proactively?

We can master the framework with practice; we simply need the discipline to apply it. Sustained success can be achieved by continuous improvement and consistently making quality decisions.

GPA PRINCIPLES—CONTENT QUALITY

Goal:

- Always start with the goal. Keep it in view at all times, and communicate it clearly, consistently, and frequently.
- Unite the team through the shared goal.

Priorities:

- Always cover the baseline first.
- Know what is more important, and do the most important thing first.

Alternatives:

- Generate multiple alternatives, then start with the best available one—the one that generates the best consequences.
- Everything is subject to change in the face of a better alternative.

IPO PRINCIPLES—PROCESS QUALITY

Information:

- Use information to measure your decision proactively, validate assumptions, measure progress, and make timely adjustments.
- Beware of half-truths.

People:

- Know who are the real decision makers, supporters, and participants.
- Involve them proactively to increase decision quality and the odds of successful implementation.

Objective reasoning:

- Responsible leaders are prepared for execution before they make the final decision.
- A decision is not choosing an action, but choosing the consequences that an action will bring.

Bibliography

Brochner, Joel. "Why It's So Hard to Be Fair." *Harvard Business Review* March, 2006, 2–4.

Drucker, Peter F. "The Discipline of Innovation." *Harvard Business Review* May–June 1985, 157–159, 189–216.

Goleman, Daniel. "Leadership that Gets Results." *Harvard Business Review* March 2000.

Hammond, John S., Ralph L. Keeney, and Howard Raiffa. *Smart Choices*. Boston: Harvard Business School Press, 1999.

Kouzes, James M., and Barry Z. Posner. *The Leadership Challenge*. San Francisco: Jossey-Bass, 2007.

Leonard-Barton, Dorothy A., and Walter C. Swap. *When Sparks Fly*. Boston: Harvard Business School Press, 1999.

Tushman, Michael L., and Charles A. O'Reilly. *Winning Through Innovation*. Boston: Harvard Business School Press, 1997.

Index